TINY HOMES

Plans for Your Perfect Home Design and a Mortgage Free Life

(Inspiration for Constructing Tiny Homes Using Salvaged)

Robert Turner

Published By Phil Dawson

Robert Turner

All Rights Reserved

Tiny Homes: Plans for Your Perfect Home Design and a Mortgage Free Life (Inspiration for Constructing Tiny Homes Using Salvaged)

ISBN 978-1-77485-248-4

All rights reserved. No part of this guide may be reproduced in any form without permission in writing from the publisher except in the case of brief quotations embodied in critical articles or reviews.

Legal & Disclaimer

The information contained in this book is not designed to replace or take the place of any form of medicine or professional medical advice. The information in this book has been provided for educational and entertainment purposes only.

The information contained in this book has been compiled from sources deemed reliable, and it is accurate to the best of the Author's knowledge; however, the Author cannot guarantee its accuracy and validity and cannot be held liable for any errors or omissions. Changes are periodically made to this book. You must consult your doctor or get professional medical advice before using any of the suggested remedies, techniques, or information in this book.

Upon using the information contained in this book, you agree to hold harmless the Author from and against any damages, costs, and expenses, including any legal fees potentially resulting from the application of any of the information provided by this guide. This disclaimer applies to any damages or injury caused by the use and application, whether directly or indirectly, of any advice or information presented, whether for breach of contract, tort, negligence, personal injury, criminal intent, or under any other cause of action.

You agree to accept all risks of using the information presented inside this book. You need to consult a professional medical practitioner in order to ensure you are both able and healthy enough to participate in this program.

TABLE OF CONTENTS

INTRODUCTION 1

CHAPTER 1: THE TINY HOUSE REGIME 4

CHAPTER 2: CONVERTED HOMES 11

CHAPTER 3: DESIGN IDEAS 22

CHAPTER 4: THE BASICS OF WOODWORKING 32

CHAPTER 5: ENVIRONMENTAL BENEFITS 46

CHAPTER 6: THE DESIGNING OF YOUR TINY HOUSE BEFORE BUILDING 60

CHAPTER 7: ANALYZE AND ORGANIZE, NUMERATE AND ANALYZE 66

CHAPTER 8: LOCATING THE RIGHT SITE AND CONSTRUCTIONS TIPS 76

CHAPTER 9: AWARENESS: PROS AND CONS TO YOUR TINY HOUSE 82

CHAPTER 10: STRATEGIES FOR MAKING THE MOST OF YOUR SMALL BEDROOM 88

CHAPTER 11: THE GUIDELINES FOR THE DESIGN AND CONSTRUCTION OF A TINY HOME 96

CHAPTER 12: A TINY HOUSE DREAMER'S COMPLETE CHECKLIST 110

CHAPTER 13: USING SPACE EFFICIENTLY......................... 117

CHAPTER 14: PLAN FOR A TINY HOUSE........................... 123

CHAPTER 15: WHAT TO MAXIMIZE THE VALUE OF A SMALL LIVING SPACE SMALL HOUSE PLANS.............................. 133

CHAPTER 16: DESIGNING A TINY HOUSE 141

CHAPTER 17: STRATEGIES AND STRATEGIES FOR LIVING IN A SMALL HOUSE 156

CHAPTER 18: WHAT'S THE REASON FOR A TINY HOUSE? PROS AND CONS. 167

CONCLUSION... 182

Introduction

Small-sized homes are coveted by many, yet only a handful of people manage to achieve it for the rest of their lives. While it may seem wonderful in the design and construction phase could quickly go against you as you live in the "dream."

It's awe-inspiring when you watch shows such as "Tiny House Nation" and "Tiny House Living." They talk about all the benefits and a few issues that occurred during the construction process and also the adjustments they needed to make when they lived in their small apartment for a couple of months. But the real world is often different from what's seen on TV.

Do you think that a family of six living in a tiny space of 100 square feet? If the circumstances change more favorable and you are being able to afford a mortgaging loan to purchase a larger house, you can be sure the tiny home is available for auction.

If you lookup for tiny houses to purchase, you'll discover a variety all over the USA available for purchase. The captions typically say, "like new, lived in, but must sell." That is, due to some reason, the idea of going tiny was not a good idea for the property owner. Many tiny houses are now rental properties as the owners no longer would like living in such small buildings.

How can you become a member of the small home movement that has been successful? What can you do to become the person who makes it work , after you have spent anywhere from 10,000 to $100,000 for your own tiny home? You can do it by adhering to some of the fundamental guidelines that make tiny home living a viable option.

There is a lot to think about before building your dream home if you are looking to succeed. The factor that will make you successful is the moment you are considering not having a mortgage or other debt and rearranging your life to suit the "small" style you've selected.

Find out how to make your tiny living arrangements a success from planning all the way to experiencing your "dream."

Chapter 1: The Tiny House Regime

What exactly is tiny living? Do you know what exactly is the significance of tiny house movements?

In essence it's the movement in which the majority of people are reducing their home and adopting tiny homes. The average home in America has a size of around 600 square feet. Typical small or tiny houses vary from 100 to 400 square feet. There are tiny homes of all shapes, forms and sizes, and allow for more simple living in spaces which are smaller , yet more efficient.

Different people have their own reasons as to why they've joined or are joining the movement however the most well-known and well-known reasons include financial worries, a need for greater freedom and more time as well as environmental issues. The majority of people earn half or 1/3 of their weekly or monthly earnings go to renting and over the course of their lives, that's about 15 years of work. Thus, living a more compact lifestyle proves to be the only option.

Why do we have Tiny Houses?

Imagine living without charges for utilities, mortgage and rent, living without worrying about collecting the water or creating electricity. In reality that you can construct this kind of home for the price of a small amount. A debt-free life will definitely change or change your life; and lead a more fulfilling life.

Tiny homes focus on being simple, and with only everything you require but, yet, elegantly. Environmental benefits associated with living small' are of important importance over the financial and economic benefits. Smaller homes have a less environmental footprints, which generally leads to lower consumption as the consumption of natural resources by humans is reduced;

they promote more simple lifestyles. The possibility of a sustainable future is more sustainable is open.

The typical tiny houses measure around 2.4 5 meters in size and include an area for living, a bathroom with a kitchen, as well as an additional sleeping loft. The house is built to be built in a manner that is able to fit into a trailer, in order to be easy to move. This transforms home ownership and increases the ownership of a home to a whole new degree since you're able own a home without the need to purchase and own land you've parked your tiny home on. These houses are also built as self-contained or off grid with the intention of generating water and electricity.

Cheap Housing Revolution: Tiny House Movement

There are a lot of unanswered questions regarding the tiny homes movement. It is essential to find answers to these questions and this is precisely where the book can help.

The "Tiny House Movement" is also known in"the "Small house movement" is a rising settlement trend in which a large portion of the population is moving away from massive homes to smaller ones. But what is the right size for tiny? Tiny is subject to debate and opinion as all situations are relative. Most people see tiny as being a space that ranges between 65 square feet and 400 sq. feet.

The size of smaller homes is contingent on the residents' lives and the amount of people who live there The majority of small homes are located in the 400-1700 square feet range. Most of the time the most common size that people in the world of housing consider to be small is between 400-1000 square feet, but there is always a difference of personal opinion.

There isn't a great deal of significance that is associated with area as some believe that it is. The most important thing is your needs to be taken care of within your home not more. Yes, it's all inclusive of your family members, except you're not living with them.

The most important principle that this movement stands for is to be aware of every aspect of how we live our lives. This is not just about buying and consumption decisions but also the more important issues like setting objectives and achieving what we want through clearing out some of our "baggage".

Information on Housing

According to a census from 2010 2392 square feet was the typical size of homes across the U.S. This is a reduction of square footage from 2007 when 2,521 square foot was the standard size. The same chart shows that in 1973 1660 square feet were the standard size. These variations clearly show that the method of calculating or averaging these sizes isn't always the same however, it is dependent on opinion.

In reality, you can drastically decrease the likelihood of financial ruin if you're fired by cutting down on your rent. It's therefore incredibly beneficial to join in the trend and move to living small in a tiny or small-sized house. Tiny homes offer many benefits (as described later in this book). But, smaller homes can will save you time and money. In addition, they provide peace of mind as the thought of doing your part to help the environment is what makes you feel happy.

Living Big, but Living Small

Although it's as absurd as it is and as true as it is. You should take a moment to think about the issue. You can live life to the best when you live in a small or tiny house; you can you can downsize for the sake of it. Small spaces allow you live your best life by clearing out the unneeded or unnecessary items. Living small is about removing clutter from your life.

Small living not only allows you organize your home through removing pile of clutter and making it smaller , but it can also:

Make your relationships simpler

Reduce the complexity of your job or business tasks

Make it easier to manage your workout routine

Make your meals simpler

Reduce your mental attitude

Make your thoughts simpler

These small changes make a difference and can lead to a positive change for your life, either now or later.

Chapter 2: Converted Homes

While standard housing is accessible to everyone however, there are homeowners who prefer a different arrangement. For instance the 2,622 square feet surface could be plenty of empty space for a family who doesn't require it. Instead of purchasing ordinary homes in the past, a lot of Americans as well as people around the world across the globe are turning to "converted houses". For a practical person the idea of any structure or item that has not served its purpose could be converted into a home with an livable, spacious interior. This is the kind of small (small) home conversions that are gaining popularity today:

Shipping Containers

According to several sources online according to a variety of online sources, there are more than 17 million container ships distributed across the globe. A quarter of this container inventory is employed for transport. However, around 675 ship containers are lost each year. This is the information collected as recent as 2014. If it weren't for the inventive person who has come up with other ways to make use of empty shipping containers, the world could perhaps feel sad for the three-fourths that are produced by China (as and more than 600 drowning in the sea every year). But the story of homes built from shipping containers is not clear. It is not known the exact date it began, even though the use of these massive trade containers for shelter has become a global trend and common.

The first mention of shipping containers for shelters is from 1965. Insbrandtsen Company Incorporated filed a patent that was titled Combination of a of a showcase and a shipping container. The idea behind the patent is to utilize shipping containers as a mobile display booths at commercial exhibitions. But the concept to use shipping containers to create homes was only introduced just a few years later, and was the brainchild of an British architect by the name of Nicholas Lacey. The 1970s were when he wrote his thesis at the university that advocated using shipping containers as an alternative suitable housing. After about ten yearsof research, an American architect by the name of Phillip Clark fine-tuned Lacey's ideas and offered a viable blueprint for a cost-effective home conversion. Patent 4854094, also known as Patent 4854094, which is also known as the Method of changing one or more shipping containers into a living spaces, was given in 1987. It was the first method for changing shipping containers into affordable and sturdy home.

A typical shipping container comes with the standard dimensions which is about 20' in height, and 8 feet wide. It is hardly ever able to exceed that 400 sq. feet limitation of a small home. So, a shipping box is often a great design for a tiny (micro) home because of its limited size. But, the frequently impractical constraints of one shipping container allow builders to use at the very least two to create a more living indoor space. As a livable home each has many advantages and disadvantages.

One of the main benefits of choosing shipping container houses is the efficiency of the price aspect. In comparison to purchasing a typical home in a suburban area the purchase and renovation of the shipping container is substantially more affordable. The owner can eliminate the costly monthly mortgage costs for the home and the lot. Although renting an apartment can be an option that appears to be less expensive but apartment units are not owned. The cost of ownership over the long term (let's say, twenty years) is a nightmare in comparison to what can be purchased with a single transaction.

Another advantage to living inside shipping containers is the fact that they are ecological and resource-efficient. In the United States and all other countries that are competitive in the market the bulk purchase of shipping containers is not enough to can cover the cost of their actually used. Converting them into homes resolves the issue of abandoned shipping containers. As opposed to traditional houses they can be used to save the the natural resources needed to build shipping container houses.

Finally shipping containers are designed for their durability. Because of its ability to withstand the pressure of kinetics and temperature, these homes offer optimal protection against weathering. Container homes made of shipping containers are durable and durable due to having a multi-story layout in comparison to traditional structures.

While the benefits are significant however, it is important to think about its negatives. Aside from that, the shipping container is made only of steel. This creates temperature control to be an issue that is extremely challenging for homeowners. An enormous amount of time and energy is typically devoted to maintaining the perfect climate in this kind of home that has been converted. If it's not the temperatures, homeowners who purchased a less version will need to contend the rust that causes many to put a large amount of money in its interior remodeling. In addition Shipping containers weren't intended to be used for long-term living. The vapors produced by the chemicals used to make the shipping containers are dangerous for health of the.

It is important to be aware that some shipping containers have been used before and the splatters and chemical residues left over after the commercial transport could be hazardous. The purchase of a shipping container for small homes is a bargain but significant expenditures in renovation and face-lifts are required to make a comfortable and comfortable interior.

Army Huts

Necessity is the source of all inventions. As history has proven there is no man-made phenomenon that has the power to create such urgency than war. Even with all its horrors the war has often transformed the way that humanity has lived. It improved standards of health care faster. The war also enabled engineers to create more advanced methods of transport. Particularly in the case of the revolutionary shelters even war has brought to its own kind of utilitarian innovation.

In World War I, the countries that were allied with France as well as the United Kingdom was at war with Germany. In the event that one of the French villages suffered the effects of German artillery German artillery England had sent its finest natural engineers to offer support.

Lieutenant Colonel Peter Nissen designed a shelter which is robust, yet simple and easy to construct. Nissen Huts are extremely simple to build. Nissen Huts became the first prototype for the semi-cylindrical cross-section army shelter that was used by the military throughout World War I up to the present. It was claimed the Nissen Huts are so easy to construct that it takes about four hours for six people to construct, and all the necessary materials can be stuffed into a single 3ton truck. The revolutionary design brought Nissen the equivalent to US $19,000 (a substantial sum for the period).

In World War II, the Nissen Huts have come to the attention of the allies United States navy engineers. They inherited the design of their British allies but wanted to make something bigger and more robust. Quonset Huts were Quonset Huts were first made in the region of their name of Quonset Point, Rhode Island. In contrast to those of the Nissen Huts predecessor,

Quonset Huts weren't limited to being used as sleeping area. They have become any kind of functional construction to accommodate all of the United States armed forces such as bars, mess halls and offices, perhaps even an armory. About 153,000 Quonset buildings were constructed through The United States navy.

After the war at the end of the war, at the end of the war, the United States economy is on its course to constant expansion and growth. But there was a distinct problem with housing for returning military personnel. There weren't enough houses to be found and the current rate of development in real estate was not able to catch up to the massive demand. In the end the discharged military engineers started changing their excess Quonset Huts to shelter the homeless veterans returning home. This was the most effective solution for the time, since extra shelter was sold at a just $2700 (since this process involves deconstruction and recycling is more expensive and labor-intensive). This helped make the transition to civilian life much more easy. The positive feedback from the residents has enabled to the US Public Housing Authority to create various communities of Quonset Huts located on the edges of urban areas.

It is believed that the Nissen as well as the Quonset Huts possess their unique design that is an advantage. The arching hull offers excellent air-flow buffer and structural stability. Because these huts for the army are constructed mostly of galvanized steel, the homes can withstand a substantial amount of physical force (exactly as they were designed by the army to support itself in the overall battle scenario). Additionally, these huts for soldiers also have the advantage of being weather-proof and provide excellent insulation for the interiors , and also preventing the possibility of leaks that are common in traditional buildings.

The first Quonset Huts may not pass as a tiny home because of its normal 720 square feet size. But, the sizes have been flexible since its introduction to the general public. These military huts are among the strongest and reliable houses ever built within the 21st Century. They've been consistently manufactured and distributed over the last 60 years.

Chapter 3: Design Ideas

A few people purchase floor plans from experienced tiny house designers, while others are happy with free plans they discovered online. Of course, you must go the "free" way initially, but if nothing is appealing to you, opt for a professionally designed one.

However regardless of whether or not you decide to purchase an idea or getting on it these suggestions can help you figure out exactly what you're looking for before moving onto the actual design process.

Draw an Floor Plan

Making your floor plan to scale is crucial and requires tools to ensure accuracy of the overall layout, which includes furniture and fixtures. To determine the scale of your measurement first, draw the width and length you've chosen for your small house using graph paper.

Note the squares per inch on the graph paper. Next, take note of how many squares per width and length your graph paper contains and then multiply them by a number to determine the total squares. Next, use these limits to figure out how many squares are in a square foot. You can also use a computer program to sketch out your floor plan easily.

After you've prepared the tools, it is now time to sketch your exterior wall of your small home, taking into account the thickness of your walls. The average thickness ranges from 4 1/2 and 6 1/2 inches, so you need to bring the drawings to scale, based on the measurements you've made.

After you have completed your exterior walls in place, it is time to choose the location you would like your door and windows to be. It is based on the dimensions of the windows and doors you've chosen. The majority of tiny home builders have already procured the materials ahead of time to reduce costs and even include the existing measurements of the materials into their floor plans. The windows are drawn in double lines and doors are drawn as a single lines and drawn as fully open using an arch. Be sure that the furniture you want to use is able to pass into the door later.

In order to design an outline of your floorplan, create your list of the most important elements you would like to see to have in your tiny home first. This includes the bathroom, kitchen or living space as well as sleeping space. Once the windows and doors are drawn in it is now possible to divide the space between the various major aspects. Consider the dimensions and dimensions of the components you'll be installing. In this scenario it is important to know what you'd like to accomplish for each room. For instance, if your goal is to have a big kitchen, you might prefer to allocate the biggest part of your square feet. But, if you desire to build a bathtub in your bathroom, this means that you'll need to adjust your plans.

Remember that the loft space isn't a part of this restriction and is typically utilized as a sleeping space. Consider the amount of headroom you feel at ease with in the loft and choose an arrangement that doesn't make you hunch and feel squeezed.

Once you've decided on the various spaces within your tiny home You should decide on the size and length of the fixtures that are built-in to these spaces, starting from the bathroom and kitchen. Find out where you can purchase smaller versions of sinks, and also if you are able to trim down the regular counters to free up space. Refurbished toilets, sinks, gas ranges and other appliances made by RVs, for example can be great fixtures built-in for small homes.

Make your own design

When you are planning the layout of your tiny home make sure to take into consideration the weather and climate of your residence. If you plan to reside in an area with severe weather conditions, then you must consider the cooling and heating system. The flow of air into and out of the home should be a part of the design too and especially in the event that you don't want to turn your tiny house in to an oven. Be sure to ensure that your home will not end up falling apart if the area is prone to severe rains, snowstorms or even hail.

The next step of the process of designing is to choose the house's "theme." The main aspects to take into consideration include the area of your tiny home and the size and the type of materials you'll use and, of course, your life style. There are tiny homes with a warm, log cabin-like feel constructed mostly of wood, and left unpainted to maintain appeal to the natural appearance. Modernized versions make use of shipping containers and include more metal and glass to reflect a minimalist urban style. There are some interesting, quirky homes that have a attractive, though unusual style. They are usually constructed from reused materials, which dramatically decrease the total cost.

The biggest challenge when designing your small home is the utilization of space. Everyone doesn't want to feel cramped even if your tolerance to small areas is large. Space efficiency is essential and therefore, make your rooms and furniture multi-purpose , and do not forget to make use of outdoor space too. Slider walls, as opposed to doors, are ideal for tiny houses because they remove any "swinging space" taken up by doors. Instead of walls that are solid you could consider curtain room partitions in your small home If you don't like snazzy styles, keep things tidy and easy!

Tiny House, Big Space Ideas

Being able to create your small house feel less cramped is an art in itself. If you're still not certain of what you can do to help make your small house appear larger and more airy, here are some fantastic ideas to incorporate into your interior design:

Install glass doors and big windows.

Glass doors and windows let light be able to enter and decrease your consumption of energy. Also, you allow the outside to be visible inside this will prevent your tiny home from feeling cramped within.

Paint with light colors, if you don't have white paint.

Light colors reflect more light, giving the room a feeling of spaciousness. Select soft hues to add an element of character to your room like pastels. Dark colors can also be a great choice provided they are used in accent objects. You could also opt for an unichromatic palette (such as using your favorite color but with different hues) to give the room an overall, uniform appearance in contrast to the overwhelming feeling created by the variety of colors.

Opt for multi-purpose, space-saving furniture.

There are a lot of furniture and appliances that can be used for multiple purposes today. Most popular are convertible sofa beds as well as the ottoman chairs which are utilized as storage boxes as well as the fold-down table stackable chairs and tables, staircases which double as storage spaces and more. You can buy the items or set them up within the small home itself.

Install shelves near the ceiling.

If you can you can, leave the floor uncluttered. That's why when you live in a small house vertical storage is crucial. Wide shelves that hang near the ceiling are the preferred choice of homeowners with small homes due to two reasons. It lets them access their things quickly without having to open the doors of cabinets. In addition, it requires them to look at exactly how many things they have on their shelves, which forces them to reduce the items they have once they begin to become clutter.

Choose one large piece instead of several smaller ones.

A smaller space will appear more unified If there's one big piece of furniture instead of a few smaller pieces which can make it appear messy. It's also helpful to pick furniture with legs that are exposed because they will provide greater floor space. Additionally it makes cleaning your floor a lot easier.

If you are unsure, use the glass or Lucite materials.

Lucite and Glass materials can not only let more light into your space, but they can also make the room appear much more sleek. They are also a sure method to make your small home look contemporary and minimalist.

Make use of mirrors for accent pieces.

The best way to make your small house appear bigger is to make use of mirrors. Mirrors reflect light and reflect the space back creating the illusion of more spacious.

There are a lot of different ideas and designs you could look at. Explore every bit of information that you can find on the internet and in books, and then apply them to come up with the best feasible tiny home design your budget and resources allow. Every minute and effort you spend on your plan will result in the results that resonate with you.

Chapter 4: The Basics of Woodworking

The construction of a tiny house requires the use of woodworking tools. Of course, you could purchase your own table or bed, however, the majority of furniture pieces sold at the department stores are made for homes built in the traditional style. If you've got woodworking abilities, you can make any furniture that meets your requirements.

At beginning, carving a piece of wood may seem an overwhelming task. There are a lot of things you have to know - from choosing the proper tools to figuring out the different types of wood you can work with. But, don't get at all discouraged by your the process of learning. Remember that even the most skilled woodworkers have to keep learning to keep up with the ever-changing times. Once you've mastered the fundamentals, you'll be able to tackle any woodworking project easily. To assist you this comprehensive guide to teach you the most crucial woodworking tips.

Safety Rules

Making a dining table from wood using your hands can be a pleasurable and rewarding experience so when you follow security precautions. The majority of these safety measures can be considered common-sense, however it is possible to overlook them if you get too excited by your work.

Remember that you should not be reckless in the woodshop. If you adhere to these security measures Your new hobby is sure to be more enjoyable.

1. Make sure you have safety equipment. This is a must for any project which involves equipment. Hearing protectors and earbuds are a must if you're working with loud equipment.

Gloves made of latex, for instance, ensure that your hands are safe and clean when working with paints and other finishes. To keep wood chips from harming your eyes wear safety glasses.

2. Dress appropriately - As with any physical exercise, be sure you are wearing the appropriate clothes to be secure. As a general rule do not wear clothing that are loose fitting because they could get caught

when cutting with a saw. It is possible to wear comfortable clothes but ensure that they protect your body from the flying chips of wood. Also, do not wear jewelry such as necklaces and bracelets.

3. Shut off appliances before changing blades. To protect yourself it is safer to remove the plug from your device first. Do not do the simple task of pressing the off button as the switches could malfunction.

4. Make sure you use the same extension cord for all your tools. This will require you to disconnect your tools when you're not making use of it. It's also a great method of ensuring you remember to unplug power tools whenever you change the blades or bits.

5. Use only sharp bits and blades- No This isn't an attempt to slice the hand into two while working with wood. If you're an experienced professional, you be aware of the dangers to use tools that aren't sharp. If the saw's blade isn't razor-sharp it will

take longer cutting the wood slab into two halves. This could cause the saw to close. Additionally, the more sharp blades result in a smoother cut, allowing you to install the hinges correctly. Be sure your blades are clean and free of pitch.

Wood Types and Species to be used

1. Oak - It is a well-known type of wood which is typically employed in the construction of furniture sets. There are many varieties of oak to test, but most of them share the same features. It has a distinct look that is suitable for most homes.

2. Maple-Maple trees are famous for their incredible endurance. If you apply the right finish to the wood, it will give off an elegant look. Like oak, you could also make use of maple to create an eating table or bench.

3. Poplar - Whether you're trying to make a wooden stool or a small bookcase You can absolutely make use of poplar for all your woodworking requirements. Being a wood is a solid material, it will last for a long time and work well when painted. Since it's inexpensive and easy to obtain, this kind of material is great to strengthen structures.

4. Pine - This is a kind of softwood that can be purchased in home stores. Long-leaf pine is a well-known type of pine that is great for furniture pieces.

5. Ipe Ipe - This natural material is a product of Brazil is well-known for its strength and water resistance. It is frequently utilized as a decking material.

6. Hickory: If you're an avid fan of baseball you might remember Hickory as the substance used to construct Babe Ruth's baseball bat. But what many are unaware of is that the family of hickory comprises many species. While all varieties of hickory are tough, they possess specific characteristics that might meet the needs of your individual. Because of its durability it isn't easy to cut even using an edger.

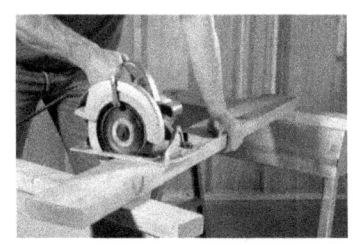

7. Beech - This wood has an uninspiring quality. While it doesn't look distinctive, beech is still a great choice when you are looking to develop your creativity. It is also possible to stain the timber to create artistic pieces appear more expensive.

Tools for trade

Here's a list of the tools needed for woodworking:

Hand Tools

1. Claw hammer is among the most flexible kinds of hammers due to it's

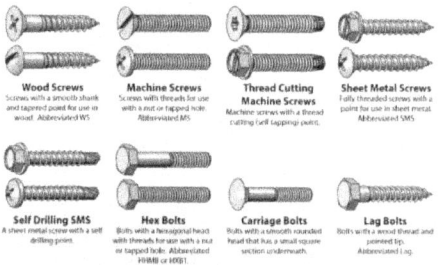

slightly round heads. The claw, however it can be used to take nails out.

2. Tape measure - Pick the retractable model for portability and easy use. The

best tape measure is marked for both metric and standard systems. Also, it should have an opening and hook. It should have a hook that is loose to allow you to be more precise in the measurements.

3. Layout square - Also referred to as a rafter or rafter square this hand tool is precise in marking the square lines every time you cut an end.

4. The utility knife is a useful tool is employed to mark stock wood and clean hinges.

5. Chisel Use a chisel remove joints or mortises.

6. Screwdrivers - Ensure that your toolbox contains each of Philips along with Flathead screwdrivers inside your toolbox.

7. Hand saws - This tool can be useful when you need to cut things quickly without the requirement of making it straight. Since these tools aren't driven by electrical energy, they require an amount of muscle power to use it.

Power Tools

1. Circular saw: You can utilize this saw by clamping it to cut fiberboard and plywood in half. It's one of the most economical and flexible kinds of saws you can purchase on the market.

2. Power drills are available in corded and cordless versions.

3. Jigsaw Make use of this tool to cut corners and make circular marks on wood.

4. Table saw is ideal for cutting large chunks of wood.

Essential Woodworking Skills You Need to Learn

1. What screw should you choose?

The majority of woodworking projects require you connect two wood slabs together, so you'll need screws. The most commonly used types include sheet metal as well as drywall, machine screws and wood screws.

The first has a rough texture and flat head. Its pitch can be rough to ensure that it holds the wood pieces to each other.

Screws made of sheet metal tend to be small and self-tapping. Drywall screws are big and more coarse as wood screws. Machine screws are, however are made of fine threads and sturdy bodies.

2. Sanding

Sanding is a procedure that involves the removal of splinters and burs. There are various tools to accomplish this.

The cheapest option will be the hand sander which is great for small woodworking projects.

The other of sander is called an orbital which makes use of discs to smooth wood surfaces. The compact design is perfect to sand tight areas.

The third kind can be described as a belt sander, the most powerful kind of sander you can buy. This tool is great for polishing large wooden surfaces that need to be finished.

Each of these sanders require Sandpaper. The product comes in different sizes and grits as well as levels of coarseness.

3. Painting

The most popular types of pain you can choose from are oil-based and latex. The latter is used intended for general use and it is simple to remove it by washing it with soap and warm water.

Paint that is oil-based however is able to adhere to various surfaces. It is ideal in the event that your initial coating of paint oil-based. Be aware that this kind of paint can be difficult to clean compared to latex paint.

Once you've decided on the type of paint, you must consider the degree of sheen. You can pick an unidirectional sheen to cover flaws on surfaces or a shiny one to provide long-lasting durability.

Chapter 5: Environmental Benefits

Tiny Homes might be small however their benefits are huge! For many living in a tiny home means financial security and for some it is the freedom to move and be able to live wherever they want at any time they'd like. There are who care about the environment more than to their pocket. It's not necessary to be hippie-style or a tree-hugger to realize that we consume far more resources from the earth than can be substituted. When we witness the signs of climate change, depletion of our ozone layer, and the tragic loss of our wildlife, there's no wonder that those who care about the environment are shifting their focus towards Tiny Homes. It's pretty eye-opening how the amount the Tiny Home saves and protects our planet.

If you're considering the possibility of buying the idea of a Tiny Home, maybe the following information will help overcome some of the obstacles and consider giving it a go. Not just are Tiny Homes tear down personal expenses, but they also reduce the effects of is caused by construction waste, lumber squandering and the excessive emissions of CO_2 into the environment. Let's look at this in a little more detail let's get started.

Tiny Homes Minimize Construction Waste

Around 40% of the planet's trash, whether in some way and another way, are created through construction. It's awe-inspiring how much an impact on waste there is when you construct a Tiny House that is between 200 and 300 square feet versus the typical home, which is about 2600 square feet. From framing to tiling roofing, sheathing and concrete, a good estimation of the waste of the Tiny Home is around 400 pounds however, you can carry around 5,000 USD of waste from a standard-sized home. The Tiny Home builders that aren't making a conscious effort to use recycled materials can experience these variations directly. Tiny Home owners could provide proof to show that an easy build can make an enormous difference in the way homes are constructed, just because of their size.

The use of timber is reduced in a Tiny House

The United States, almost three-quarters of the total use of timber every year comes from the private housing sector. Although it's great to recycle paper, it doesn't even begin to scratch the itch in the use of timber that the Tiny Home can. It requires over 90 percent more wood to construct the 2,600-square-foot home as compared to the 200-square-foot Tiny Home. Utilizing less wood is less power needed to cut or age, split and finish, store and move. What can be moved in just a few hours to construct a Tiny Home could require multiple trips over a period of time to move it onto the construction location of a conventional-sized house. Thus, the construction of Tiny Homes also saves on the cost of diesel gas and fossil fuel.

The CO_2 emissions of different countries are compared.

The emission of CO_2 into our atmosphere has caused havoc to the climate of the world and is thought to be one of one of the major players in the process of causing global warming. Although many politicians would like to make it appear that global warming isn't a thing however, science provides a completely different picture of the effects. Climate change has caused our ice caps to melt and sea levels to increase. The habitats of our wildlife are being destroyed by climate change, causing millions of species to go extinct, many others to fall on the edge of disappearing.

Nearly 18% of greenhouse gases that are released into the atmosphere come by the private housing sector at an alarming amount. A home of 3,000 square feet can release 28,000 lbs of CO_2 each year in the atmosphere of Earth and only 220 pounds of CO_2 each year for a Tiny Home. While they're small in size, Tiny Homes are incredibly efficient and consume only 914 kWh of power annually, compared to 12,773 kWh for a typical-sized home. It's not difficult to realize that the reduction in the cost of electricity, heating, as well as cooling costs of Your Tiny Home is going to be evident in your monthly budget too.

Green-friendly devices and practices

There are some things Tiny Home dwellers regularly do that allow them to be completely "off their grid" and to live in harmony with their surroundings. In most cases they don't have to be extraordinary actions that are taken by Tiny Homeowners. Rather it's their norm. We've listed some of these environmentally friendly devices and practices, so you can gain an understanding of how to enjoy the Tiny Home lifestyle.

Toilet Composting

The composting toilet can be described as a water-free system that utilizes an aerobic process to break down human excrement. The most efficient composting toilets separate urine away from solids, and then utilize an air conditioner powered by generators to dry the waste more. If the bathroom functions properly and the equipment is in good working order and functioning properly, there won't be any stink and the waste will be used to fertilize gardens or plant. Depending on how many persons reside in your tiny home The toilet will have to be cleaned up every 3 to four weeks.

While composting toilets can reduce by about $50 per month on your water bill if have a connection with city utilities, the first price of a composting toilet could be a lot more costly. The cost of flushing toilets is around $100 to $200 however, a composting toilet can cost between $1,500 and $4,000. This method is not designed to make Tiny Home residents save money, but rather to enable them to self-sufficiency and not rely on the services of the public sector.

If you are deciding on composting toilets, when you are in a city, make certain to consult with the city codes. Some ban their use within city boundaries. If you decide to compost your toilet, then it is a good option, you could dilute urine and transform it into gray water that you can use in your garden. Solid waste that has been dried could be used for this also.

Solar and Wind Power

Utilizing the earth's resources to provide power to the power of your Tiny Home is a common practice however don't believe that it's going to cost just a few dollars. It's initially more costly to build the Tiny Home using eco-friendly devices however, there's an appeal to doing it. You could reside in nothing, totally free of outside services and the costs they incur. Through time these eco-friendly devices will be able to pay for themselves and give you the liberty that only a few enjoy but when you're working with the tightest budget, it could take a long time to acquire and set up the systems.

The wind and solar cells are able to power an Tiny Home. First, you'll need to determine what size you want for your tiny House and the number of people who will reside there. You'll then need to figure out what's going to be running from within your Tiny Home. For instance, will the stove be electric or gas? What amount of water will you require to heat on the course of a typical day? The area in which you'll be staying provide enough sunlight and winds? If no, then how large generator will you require? There are a lot of questions to be answered and the answers will vary based according to the private usage or use of Tiny Home.

It is possible that you will require an solar calculator to calculate the amount of solar panels required to generate electricity. Once you've determined the amount that solar cells are needed, you can decide whether to put solar panels on top of the house or you'll require some free-standing panels. If you choose to place your solar panels, make certain to keep them out of the reach of trees and other plants that could block sunlight or harm the panels.

Based on your requirements the power of wind can be achieved through the installation of an on-the-roof wind turbine.

The following is an innovative design that features the solar cells built into the capsule that are able to cover the roof, as well as wind turbines that are attached on the inside of the. Although it's an ultra-modern design, it is currently used for research purposes and commercial offices in remote areas this could very well be the trend of the future for Tiny Home owners.

Gray Water and Rain Water Harvesting

System

A majority of places aren't going to receive enough rain to supply all the water you require every month, however an enormous amount of water could be collected prior to needing to tap into the backup source. When you're Tiny Home is going to be stationary, you may want to think about the possibility of a large cistern to store rainwater. The water requirements for a typical home are according to the following.

Per Person Drinking Water 1 Gallon

Toilet (if flushable)2 Gallons Per Flush

Shower 2 Gallons Per Minute

Of of course, this doesn't include the water you need to cook or wash your dishes, hands, and even your clothes. If we suppose that a moderate adult uses 15 gallons of water per day, this would mean around four inches of rain every month. Naturally, the amount of water needed will increase with each additional person who lives inside your Tiny Home. In the majority of places the rain does not fall every day or every month in the same way therefore it is essential to have an storage device. One of these devices is a rain cushion.

This one is big that can easily be stored outdoors in the event of rain however, you can purchase them in a variety of sizes to fit easily under the bed or in the cabinet. Because they're inflatable, they're easy to empty and to store when you're moving.

Propane Power

Propane tanks are simple to put within the Tiny Home. One thing to remember is that propane for warm climates is different from the cold-climate type. The levels of butane are higher in colder climates. It's best to use propane only in the location from where you bought it. If not, you can trade in your tanks and purchase a new one as you move. The propane tank is typically located outside the trailer or on the side of an existing stationery Tiny Home.

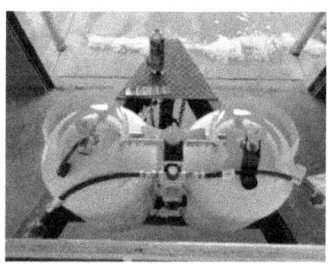

Propane is a source of power for appliances like a gas stove as well as electricity, should wind and solar power fail to suffice to heat your water. It also powers your heating and air conditioning in addition.

Building Green

When building it is important to use every repurposed and recycled items you can. To build building insulation and wood for construction and storage space in your tiny house making use of reclaimed and recycled materials can help you help protect the environment. Since your requirements will be smaller, a lot of your building materials can be sourced from bigger-sized construction websites. Contact your builder and inquire whether you can salvage materials from their projects. They will most likely be willing to assist and will are grateful for the time and money spent to transport their unused building materials to a dump for construction. (BUT do not steal materials)

These are only a few options to take into consideration when you want to be completely off the grid or go environmentally friendly as much as you can. It's easier to incorporate these items into your construction however if your budget prevents you from doing so it's possible to do small amounts at a time. Every bit of effort counts savings in resources and costs.

Chapter 6: The Designing of Your Tiny House Before Building

Making your dream home in a tiny space is among the most exciting and rewarding tasks you could ever undertake. This is due to the ease of construction that comes with it, in contrast to what is commonly believed.

The main thing you need to keep in your head is that the work can be a bit challenging at first and you may be overwhelmed.

This is often the situation when you begin to consider the expense associated with diverse construction tasks which include electrical wiring as well as the installation of appliances and plumbing, and so on.

At first it can be difficult, but the end result can be very satisfying. Making your own tiny house is well worth the duration of the project.

This is the most obvious when you see the plan take shape and beginning to tile up your home from just a tiny piece of tile to a full-scale structure that will meet your requirements. The next steps will give you the best tips to build your own tiny home.

Step 1. Designing the home

The first step to build your home is to determine the style that is most suitable for the requirements of your test. This is probably the most enjoyable aspect of building. The process requires using our human imagination and images to implement a specific method.

Here, you'll need the use of a pencil, drawing pad and our minds to create a home in accordance with the old saying that we are the masters of our own creation.

In the process of planning your house the most crucial thing that you must keep in your mind is to think about the purpose of the home. That means you need to decide if it's intended to be an apartment for vacation or as a home, or a residence. In addition the design of your house must consider the utility costs, such as the usage of solar panels that will reduce the cost of electricity, as well as other things.

Before you draw the floor plan for your house , and also the dimesions you want to draw for the tiny home It is essential that you sketch it out on a sketch paper. This is essential when you're hiring someone to help with the design of your floor plan. A few of the elements you should consider when designing include:

The dimensions and the area of the tiny homeThis means that you must know the design of the site, regardless of whether it's sloping or flat-leveled. It is also important to know if the location of your tiny home is damp or dry or swampy this will determine the kind of the foundation to be laid.

If there are massive stumps that surround the home, do they require removal, or can be constructed on top of them? And what is how many levels the house will be built on?

The design of the tiny home- this is where your design for the house is reflected. The design of your house is determined by what you'd like to achieve, and if there are any boulders in the area that could pose an obstacle to the layout of your tiny home.

Another question you must consider is whether you are using rectangles or circles, or squares that need to be incorporated in the design of the home. This includes places like porches and balconies which could alter the design of the house as well as the ability to incorporate these new shapes into your tiny home.

Its roof is the one that covers the small houseis what determines whether the roof of the home is flat or hipped, or gabled. This also includes whether the roof is covered with iron sheets or tiled.

Energy access is an important aspect that determines the layout of the home. That means that if the house is connected to energy , this could influence the characteristics of the gas system, water system and sewerage systems as well as power lines. This will also inform whether the solar panels installed in the tiny home are an appropriate choice and the necessity of connecting these to the power source.

Laundry utility - if the house layout takes into consideration the laundry facility and location, then where should the laundry room be situated within the home. Also, consider the necessity of an entrance back door and the necessity for stove or gas in this instance.

Bedrooms- the primary reason for a tiny house usually reveals the requirement for a specific quantity of rooms. That means the amount of bedrooms that meet the requirements of a small home will have an direct impact on the style of the home. It is also important to consider whether bedrooms will require integrating the presence of visitors at some point.

It is also about integrating storage spaces and closets which are adequate for those who live in the home and their items. In addition bedrooms decide if there is a requirement for a bathroom centrally located that is accessible to all or if each bedroom needs the bathroom of its own.

The size of the bed is another element that determines the layout of the small home. This implies that if there is the need for built-in beds, as well as way to access the bedroom is via an elevator, among other things.

Chapter 7: Analyze and Organize, Numerate And Analyze

In discussing the subject of de-cluttering, we rarely consider the realities that each of us experience in all their entirety. We purify, condense, and arrange our real world but not our virtual world, but rather our mind, our soul and our spirit. De-cluttering your entire body to prepare for your new tiny home begins by pondering the reason.

Look through the space you'd like to clear.

Capture it.

Shut your eyes.

Register it.

Breathe deeply.

Keep your breathing.

Re-capture it.

Consider the reason it makes you feel claustrophobic? Was it not something that stoked your enthusiasm to death in your past?

In your mind, picture the white expanse of space.

Clean.

Nothing or nothing except you, your chair , and your air!

Then, open your eyes.

Check out the mess and the four walls in your room.

First of all, you need to paint the surface white using the brush inside your head.

Now , sit down, there!

Follow the path that I'm marking out for you to follow.

Reviewing your clutter

If you're too enthusiastic Name your home.

Yes!

Name it.

The List is Down

Yes. Write down every item you own on a spreadsheet. Note them down with numbers!

Then, you can walk through the room, writing down everything. If you'd like to immediately end the task you can use the technique of Four-Boxes. Bring in four standard-sized boxes and separate them according to their purpose at current. For example, boxes with 'Yes" and "No" or with an additional of 'Maybe', or following the same pattern for how many boxes you wish to eliminate the things you've thought of as the main clutter.

Write them down, then mark them out when you've separated them.

You can get Cupboards

Get your posture back and prepare to explore. Check out your space and note how organized the cabinets within your home are DIY ideas on how to make your own cabinets and the reemphasis on the similar.

Yes. Take them!

Cupboards can help you keep your items in the most convenient distance that is clear to see.

Utilize them! There are always options our arsenal to clear our homes and make them our home!

The process of making cupboards as well as the modern and stunning light in the dark, cabinets and more, are what creative spirit is all about when it comes to decorating your small space in your home. When we look at the kind of spaces we is comfortable and happy with, we find our personal comfort levels and be awakened at the same time.

Set up your furniture and cabinets in accordance to how you've named your house!

Numeric

This is the point at which you can alter the accessibility, availability and affordability to renovate your home! The cost of what you're promised or obligated to pay for, will give you an instant incentive to get started on building your dream home.

Divide. Stop. Mark!

The gold standard of de-cluttering and making the most of your space to spread out and not be a tangled mess is the rule of God that guarantees peace, at least to some degree.

Simply take note of your possessions and then split them into groups. You must mark off what is not needed, and what the needs should be and then take care of it. There are many aspects of pleasure for oneself as one thinks how to dispose of waste, disposal as well as utility. But, one must remain true to necessity and practicality with the same sexiness in the case of Sherlock Holmes.

Depending on the amount of cabinets and boxes you will be able to name and categorize your belongings!

Exploring Waste Management through

Good Waste Management is one of the responsibilities that one must make in the present. So, if you come across things that aren't dear to you any more, but is worthless, consider the disposal capabilities of the item! Each item on the market is available and in good condition.

Be educated, get the knowledge , and master the art of be honest in your interactions with others, your love, as well!

Organise

Take a look at the space you're intending to clean Space by space. For instance, if you are looking to reduce clutter and maximize the space in your home, begin by analyzing, organizing and setting up, each room!

• Start by clearing out your bathroom.

Plan, Plot and Arrange

The second physical indication of action is part of plan and planning. Take a look at the items you own, or have purchased (or purchase it now! It's an excuse for you to take holiday!) To arrange your shelves, cupboards and wardrobe. Plan everything in the the right dimensions and functions into your mental image and mark them off!

The next step is to arrange items in your mind. Make sure to walk around with your head in a mental image, and then surround yourself with your things. The day-to-day items, the bare basic items and the interiors. From the ashtrays to the watches with diamonds, making sure you have everything organized is a sign that you are on the right track or a sense of comfort.

So, you should arrange everything in your head and move around. Examine if it's just a distraction or the best way to get what you want to go about it?

Imagine Moving

This is a quick step to help you get started in the right direction. Do not follow the interior decorating magazine, I'd suggest. Also, you need to make a smart reference to them! Through the piles of unreliable and depressing advertisements, you'll discover useful items that could seem like the ideal option to put on your table, bed or even as speakers! Let everything count .

So, I'd suggest that you should go on physically amazing holiday. Relax your mind through the shops and then renovate your house following a thorough sitting down! This will be an amazing experience!

Set it!

Once you've got everything, you can set it!

Chapter 8: Locating the Right Site and Constructions Tips

After you've completed the preliminary steps of making your tiny home but it's not yet time to apply the nail in the hammer. There are some more decisions to be made. After overcoming the legal hoops then you must decide which location you'll construct your tiny home as well as the place where you'll reside. As we've mentioned the legal requirements that differ from one place to another, so you don't just have to locate the land you want but ensure that it's a suitable land to build a tiny dwelling on it.

The land that is rural is typically the most accessible due to the lack of restrictions however, you'll be further from shopping, city services entertainment, work and employment. Be aware that the further you get to the city the less land will be , and also it will be more costly. Although you won't require lots of land to build your tiny home however, you must make sure that you have enough space to allow you to be able to live comfortably and not in the shadow of your neighbour, particularly when you are trying to get around certain laws you'll encounter when building a tiny home.

There are a variety of methods to go about getting the land you need to build your dream home. Begin by looking through on real estate websites. Be sure to ensure that the area is big enough to accommodate your small home.

If your tiny home will be mobile, then you should look for a land area that is controlled to allow camping all year round. It is not common in urban areas. You might encounter limitations that make it impossible to live in your tiny dwelling for longer then 30 days at stretch.

The purchase of land is not the only choice when it comes to choosing a suitable location for your dream home. There are other options to think about:

You can lease space in an RV park.

Buy an existing campground or trailer park and establish a tiny home community.

It can be parked in the backyard of a family member.

Be aware that because tiny homes don't meet the standards of society to live in Finding a suitable place to live in will require you to think out of the box. No matter if you want your home that is on wheels or standalone one, it is important to make sure you're staying within the parameters of the laws. However, the minds of people are changing to favor smaller structures, so at times it's as simple as communicating with government officials, and convincing them your house will add value to your neighborhood.

Basic Construction Tips

After you've found your property It's time to give some thought to the layout for your brand new home.

When you start your small home construction, begin by laying the foundation. Contrary to the construction stage of a typical house, you can opt to build a foundation in the ground similar to a traditional home, or use a mobile foundation with flatbed trailers. There are a few advantages to having a foundation that can be moved. When you're ready for a move it is easy to connect your small home to a truck , and move the entire structure. This is especially beneficial if you are concerned that you could be a victim of zoning regulations.

Whatever foundation you pick and if you do not have prior experience designing homes by yourself, it is advisable to purchase a set blueprints. It will stop you from taking a lot of wrong turns in the construction phase even if you're not an expert. There are blueprints to choose from various companies, with prices that vary from $200 to $1000. They will provide you with precise details to guarantee that your home is structurally sound.

The first thing you should purchase is your trailer. The cost of these depend on the location. They can be found for sale from $1600.00 and up based of the options you require. You may even get a secondhand one at no cost in an area salvage yard if you spend the time to look them up. If you're thinking about trailers, be sure to look up the Gross Weight Vehicle Rating (GWVR). This is the number that tells you the weight an axle can carry (including the contents). This is where purchasing plans can be useful. Even then, it's difficult in the beginning of any project to determine exactly how much the final home's weight will be.

Additionally, you need to understand the licensing requirements and get licence plates, electronic brakes brake and back up lights scissor jacks and an auxiliary hitch.

Chapter 9: Awareness: Pros And Cons To Your Tiny House

The pros of your tiny home:

Affordable. It is no secret that money is essential for the majority of people. If one is convinced that they have the ability to live a decent life and still save money it's not much more appealing than this. This is particularly the case since tiny homes that are smaller 1,000 square feet could cost less than the equivalent of 8000 sq. feet of land clearly. Additionally the list, they are also less expensive to maintain because of the lack of infrastructure and facilities of small-sized homes.

Priorities vary among people and having the mansion of your dreams might not be among the top priorities. Therefore, they prefer to reduce their expenses and invest in different locations, such as expanding their businesses, higher education and travel.

Because of their dimensions, they don't have enough space to hold lots of furniture and other things. This means that it lowers the value of your investment. A person who moves from a big home, such as a 8000 square feet of land to a small house smaller that 1000 square feet, will have the advantage of increasing their savings by quite a bit. Because of the shrinking of their land, they are able to save money on their land first , followed by the amount of possessions they'll have to dispose of in order to accommodate their tiny homes.

It's environmentally friendly since it permits you to manage it using less resources, for instance, a large house with multiple rooms would require the air conditioning or heater that consumes more energy contrasted to small homes. This is why it's an effective way of reducing energy consumption.

Smaller homes are simpler to maintain and clean because of their smaller dimensions. This helps you conserve time that you would otherwise spend the maintenance and cleaning of your home.

Small houses are usually suited to your personal taste, meaning that the tiny space must be your own personal space to your own retreat. Therefore, they provide tranquility and a sense of calm. It's your personal home, which is appealing to quite many.

Sometimes, tiny homes are constructed on wheels, such as the caravan. In this case the tiny home can be moved to wherever you like and can reduce the expense of purchasing a car.

A lot of people believe that tiny houses can provide an easy lifestyle. While it's true that you can fit just a few things in a tiny space however, it's also the case that you can integrate different luxury items more efficiently than you are at a larger home. Let's take an example here. If you're looking to have a particular design on your walls, or you want a specific type of flooring that is costly but you aren't capable of achieving it in a larger home. This is because the first investment was more than twice the cost of your home's size and the total expense will be excessive. You can still embellish your tiny home with the style you prefer and include luxuries in this manner.

The cons of your tiny home:

Certain people prefer a more luxurious life style, as opposed to the simple living that comes with small houses. It's something that is based on preference or your personal preferences.

A small house has no storage facilities. It is impossible to cram things in and out because of the limited space. Additionally, as there is no storagespace, it's difficult to store the things you need.

Many people feel that small homes are becoming suffocating because of their tiny dimensions. In addition, because the whole home is essentially the space of a small area and some people are annoyed to find the kitchen situated in the same space as the bedroom, and the bathroom is just a few steps away.

A tiny home could be perfect for a single person or one couple. However, it isn't suitable for an extended family. There can be a lot of people and this can be a hassle.

Privacy is diminished if two people live together, or two or more people sharing. This isn't optimal for some individuals since the majority of people want being in control of their privacy.

It is possible that you will not be able to host guests in the space you have. Therefore, inviting guests over for a celebration might not be as fun for everyone as it might appear.

Certain people are especially interested in gardens and gardening. In a small home it is unlikely that you will be able to have the garden. This is why people do not want to live in tiny homes. But, you could opt to find a acceptable compromise and build your home near a park or an area that is green. This will give you beautiful views from your windows.

If you're interested primarily gardening, you could decide to grow small plants in your window to satisfy your passion for gardening , but require less care. But, if you're not ready for the task, small homes might not be the best option for you.

Chapter 10: Strategies for Making the Most of Your Small Bedroom

Maintain your bedroom's order and relaxed by following these suggestions and techniques:

36. Deep headboard

Your bed's headboard must not only be used to rest your head. With a headboard that is deep can be used to put away cushions, sheets, or pillows. Make sure to keep the storage function in mind, and you will be no random objects strewn across your bedroom. Get what you'll need and put away the remainder.

37. Shut the bedside tables

There's no need to fill up the bedroom space that isn't being used by putting up those old-fashioned bedsides tables. If you require reading lamps, opt for those with a curved design that are fixed to the walls. If you're looking to have some space to store things you can get a wall-mounted shelves or a mobile standing pedestal that is able to be positioned wherever in the space.

38. Smaller footprints

Maintain your bedroom tidy by using pieces that can hold the most with small footprints. If the floor is clear to the eyes it appears open and spacious. It is also possible to increase the vertical dimension of the room in this manner.

39. Clothing, the problem

Bedrooms are often plagued by the problem of being overcrowded with clothes. To prevent this from happening avoid this, don't accumulate your closet in a way that is unnecessary. Save what you need and then donate the rest. Do not keep your Once-upon-a-time-favorite dresses stashed hoping that you'll eventually fit in them once again. If you're not able to fit into these dresses now, simply remove them from the closets of your bedroom.

40. Beddingsmania

I am sure that bedding is thought of as a major source of clutter. You can store your bedding in secluded bed boxes. The slim beds made from iron wrought certainly enhance the look of the house however they lack many storage options. Therefore, choose beds with drawers or boxes, and the issue of where to put your bedding solved.

41. Back-of-door hangers

Install slim hangers at the back of your bedroom's door. Because every inch is important, this will aid greatly for more wardrobe storage. Find attractive hangers and hooks to will enhance your style.

42. Cubed Settees

If you'd like to include an option for seating for your bed, invest in cubicle settees that are able to hold items that are used regularly. Your guests will not be aware that the bright and colorful cubicle settees positioned in front of your bedroom's windows hold pillows covers and more. It's fascinating!

43. Make the wall your own

Other than the typical images or paintings wall surfaces in your bedroom can be decorated with a variety of useful and cosmetic features. Choose utilitarian boxes that are attractive and large. Combining them, you can decorate the walls in a creative way to show the appearance of a master designer.

44. Divide and rule

The large, deep drawers can mix everything you want to keep. Find decorative dividers that can organize the drawers. Place smaller or trays in your closet for bedroom storage or on tables at your bedside and throw things into them rather than on your mattress.

45. Let them know!

Get hooks or hangers that are slim and hang them on your closet or close to the headboard of your bed. Then hang them over all your fashionable caps, belts, scarves and neckpieces, as well as earrings, daggers, etc. The hooks and hangers can display your collection, and also free storage space within your closet. Because they're easily prominent, you'll be able select the hangers and hooks more quickly.

46. Door-to-door dressing table

Reduce space usage by installing an entire length mirror in front of the door of your bedroom, along with transparent bags. The bags with transparent lids will allow you to access everything you need for your makeup while you dress yourself the mirror. There is no need for a separate dressing table that occupies an entire corner in the space. If the door is shut the mirror installed will reflect light and create a feeling of greater size and spacious.

47. Pockets to charge phones

Don't leave your phones close to your bed while they charge. Create a phone stand out of a plastic sheet or clear bag that is put over the charging socket. This will prevent the user from getting on their phones or falling over the charging wires.

48. Consider investing in a murphy bed

A bed made of murphy is a multi-tasking furniture that can be used for multiple purposes. In the evening, it functions as it's a bed and during daytime, it could be put in the wall as an efficient cabinet. Many homeowners choose to use murphy beds in guest rooms however their usage has expanded to a tiny master bedrooms. Yes, it will be difficult to lift it up and lower it down and down, but think of it as an exercise!

49. Floating shelves

Shells in the walls offer more than just a way to organize your stuff and can be used to create. A majority of floating shelves feature unique designs and colors, which means their design is versatile.

50. The wonders of wall-mount

Wall-mounted cabinets may be the most space-saving among cabinets. Instead of eating up space due to their size walls, wall mounted cabinets and closets give you lots of room to move around. As a last tip do not forget to make use of the space beneath your hanging clothes. They could serve as a storage space. Also, don't forget install a mirror on your cabinet!

51. The carpet was soiled.

While they're a well-known as an interior design icon, having carpets within the bedroom may make it appear much smaller. The secret to this is that when you are able to see the flooring (without clutter naturally!) The room appears more spacious. Your eyes will see the carpet as a squishy material. Carpets that are swept away also mean less stress about cleaning it.

52. What about the ceiling?

If you're planning to incorporate the look of your bedroom, don't focus too much on the walls! Be aware that they will be used to store other items. Remember that you have your ceiling. It's true that you don't need to be an artist to design it. There are a lot of peel-it and stick-it wall murals in the home decor stores!

Chapter 11: The Guidelines for The Design and Construction of A tiny home

Since the cost of housing has been climbing over the last few years, living in tiny houses has become more sought-after. Many people prefer living in small houses for a long time, while others build these as retreats. They are simple structures that are both efficient and financially feasible. Numerous organizations across the globe have begun to build these homes to aid people who are homeless or struggling financially. If you are considering building the possibility of building a small home for yourself, it is important be aware of certain issues in your mind and develop the necessary knowledge. A house is a complex structure that is built regardless of the size and requires precision.

Take a look at the Local Laws

Different regions or states have different laws in relation to small houses. It is important to research the safety standards established by the housing department of your particular state. Be sure to adhere to all the guidelines and policies. Check with them prior to you begin building or designing your home to avoid costs or further work later on. Many tiny home owners build their homes on trailers to get rid of the burden getting building permits. The majority of these houses come with wheels, which allows them to be classified as a campervan, instead of an illegal tiny home. It is important to know local laws, as they can differ from one location to another. This is especially true when you're building or moving to another state.

The law can give you an idea of the size you are allowed to build as well as the rules for any material that can be employed. Also, you must determine which areas can construct or even park the tiny home. In California tiny foundation houses must adhere to regulations of the Department of Housing and Commercial Development rules and regulations, and also be registered in accordance with the California Building Code.

In terms of dimensions, a house is considered to be a tiny in California in the event that it is smaller that 400 square feet. Tiny homes can be constructed on a foundation or with wheels in this state. A home on wheels must be classified as a vehicle for recreational use. The laws governing zoning in California also prohibit purchasing land in a variety of places to build tiny homes. If you construct your home near the ocean it is required to belong to a tiny-house community.

A well-planned plan is essential.

The design of your home is crucial. This is particularly true for small houses. Every square inch in tiny houses must be used in the most efficient way that is possible. If you plan it with care and prudence your small home will appear larger than it really is. A careful plan will create a home that is more comfortable to live in. The use of sliding doors is a method of making the most of space. Traditional swinging doors can consume space and may restrict the space available to work in. The maximization of window space is an important factor to consider when making plans. Make sure that you design your home in a manner that plenty of natural light is able to enter and that the house is in close proximity with the outside to create an illusion of more space.

Don't shrink everything

If you're reducing on the dimensions of your house it doesn't mean you have to reduce everything. There is no need to buy an exact replica of the things you'd like to fit into the home. If, for instance, you attempt to reduce the size of your bed excessively it could hinder sleeping well and make you uncomfortable. A bathroom that is too small could also affect the quality of daily life at home. Instead, you should concentrate on making the bathroom more practical.

Multi-functionality is crucial for a small home. Find furniture that can be able to double as a bed, for instance couches that fold out to become a bed, or a table that can be used that can be used for dining serves as a double purpose. You could even build your walls so to allow them to be pulled up for seating or pulled back when not being used. There are endless options if you choose to design a unique architecture for your small home. It is important to think outside of the box and not rely on the same design approach like traditional homes. It's simple to have enough space in a huge house however, you must find space for a small home.

Make sure you prioritize your Foundation and the Roof.

The foundation of a house must be strong. It is important to build the base in a manner that the home can move easily. This gives you the flexibility to move your home should you need to change your location for work or for any other reason. A further benefit of constructing homes on trailers is that you are that it allows you to get around the legal issues related to foundation homes.

Apart from building your home using wheels may also build it on stilts, beams, skids, posts or even the cement slab foundation. It is important to think about your requirements for your house when you select the best foundation for it. The roof is an additional aspect to consider when designing. A flat roof can result in issues with debris or water accumulation. Sloping roofs are essential in areas that experience an excessive amount of snowfall or rainfall. It is important to consider the weight of snow too. If you are planning to move frequently when you are home, you must take into consideration the various places, not just the one in which you're building your home.

Take into consideration the weight

The weight is an important aspect to think about when designing your home. The entire house has to be built using lightweight materials, making it simple to move. If the house is built on a trailer, the torque weight must be taken into consideration. This is the amount of weight at on the sides of your trailer in comparison to the weight in the rear. It must be sufficient weight in the front of the trailer to ensure that it doesn't sway during transport. If the vehicle's weight is lower than the vehicle's weight, it can sway between the sides. In the event that the amount of weight is excessive and it causes over-load on the tires and cause a push onto the vehicle. It could result in a tense and potentially dangerous situation.

The planning and execution of the building in a manner that puts the proper weight on both sides is essential to ensure safety.

Utilize Different Materials

The materials used in traditional home are usually tough and heavy. For small homes it is necessary to use a lighter materials. As a minimalist, it is recommended that you must also think about choosing materials that are eco-friendly. Recycling old materials or materials can help you save dollars. Architects are becoming more flexible and creative when they are using recycled materials nowadays. You can consult or hire someone who can help you through this option for your small home.

The selection of the material you choose is vital since every single surface within your house should be counted. Glass is the best choice as a window, however there are various kinds of glass that you should consider. The thermal properties of glass must be taken into consideration based on the climate in which you reside. It is possible to reduce the cost of energy substantially by using appropriate materials in your home and. Look for ways to let natural cooling or heating instead of relying on energy sources. This will let you reduce your carbon footprint, too.

Software

There's a wide range of software available that lets you to design your own designs prior to execution. Although some are free, others may cost you some money. Certain software programs are simple to use, but they may not provide a lot of information. However, some of the more complicated applications permit you to create detailed designs. Here are some fantastic software programs you can utilize to create your own home:

Floorplanner

It is an easy-to-use software online that lets you to design and publish flooring plans on the internet. It's ideal for planning the layout of your small home. It can be easily implemented even if you already have some concepts. There are a variety of ideas to test out.

The Sims 4: Sims 4

It's possible to be shocked at first, but it's real. This game simulates fun but also effective in helping you create your own home. Its only downside is that you cannot print the designs you create within the game. You can however test a variety of design options for the exterior and interior which will provide an idea of what you'd like your small home to appear.

SketchUp

SketchUp is a free application which you can download and later upgrade to paid plans. It's a stand-alone program, however it was originally owned by Google. The majority of architects and builders use this program because it is very sophisticated. However, it's not as user-friendly for novices and you'll have learn how to making use of it properly. However, it is one of the most highly advised softwares for creating small-sized houses.

Sweet Home 3D

This program is designed primarily to design interiors. Floor plans can also be created using this software but it's better for interiors because of the 3D-view. There are numerous furniture options along with other features for interiors. It lets you customize the plans of your home quite significantly. It is much easier to utilize than SketchUp. If you want to plan your day it is recommended to use floor planner.

Planner 5d

The software online is compatible with mobile devices, too. The accessibility to the software is a benefit of this program since many others require a computer. It permits you to change between 2D floor plans to 3D exteriors and interiors.

SketchUp allows you to complete the task with greater detail and Planner 5D lets you get it done while in motion.

HomeByMe

Another browser-based program which allows you to draw 2D floor plans using. Furniture can be placed making use of 3D model. However it is true that the 3D model isn't very useful with this software and is merely something you can make use of for a general concept of design. The software is available at no cost and utilized without charge for 3 projects. Then, you'll need to pay for packs based on the amount of designs you'd like to design.

Chief Architecture

It is a professional software. It's geared towards an audience of professionals like architects working in the construction industry. It's expensive and also, however, you could invest in it if you own an insignificant home company or simply would like to test it. It works on Windows and iOS.

Punch Home

Punch Home is also a paid program, but it is cheaper than Chief architect. It lets you create extensive designs. It's an excellent choice following Floorplanner, a simple program which you can use to create the most basic designs. It allows you to design 2D and 3D designs with great detail using this program. Start with simple features before moving on to more complicated ones once you are more comfortable with this program.

AutoCAD

AutoCAD is a popular software by experts and architects. It's on the costly side, yet it allows you to create stunning tiny house designs. Consider investing in this product if you are interested in computer-aided design as you design your small home. If you are only interested in the look of a single home, the cost could be too expensive.

Draftsight

It is a good program that is fairly new and is currently in beta stage, making it difficult to use. But, it's extremely powerful and offers numerous options.

Try any of the software mentioned above to design your small home designs.

Chapter 12: A Tiny House Dreamer's Complete Checklist

Have you been enticed to move to a smaller home? Don't open your wallet yet. Before you begin purchasing your items, study this chapter and discover the most important things you'll require to know when you plan to begin living in a tiny house.

Space

The first step is that you'll need to think about the size of the area you'll require to build your home. Remember that houses are considered to be small when they have floor space smaller than 400 square feet. (Other "tiny homes" can be as large as 500 sq. feet however, the standard size is limited to 400 sq. feet.) To determine how much space you'll require for your house take into consideration the number of persons who are expected to live in the space , as well as the quantity of belongings they have and require often. If you intend to live in a single-person home, you can consider purchasing an apartment as little in size as 100 square feet. If you have a small family of several teens or little children, the largest dimensions of the home might be required for everyone to be comfortable. Don't convince yourself that you don't require certain items in order that you can fit them into the smallest space. If the majority of things that you own are actually necessities make sure you have as much living space possible.

Floor plan

A number of small house websites offer floor plans to interested homeowners. But , given the sheer number of floor plans available what can you do to decide which one to choose? To answer this first issue, you should consider the following points below.

Do you have plans to cook in the confines of your home? Do you consider having a kitchen an option?

Do you need a bath?

Do you have pets?

How can you make the most of storage space in an incredibly small home? (Answers to chapter 4!)

What number of bedrooms do you require? Are you ready to build lofts?

Have you got any passions that require their own space?

Have you got any need in terms of space?

After you have answered these questions then you are now able to assign rooms of your tiny home.

Wheels or none

In Chapter 1 that a lot of tiny homeowners decide to build their homes on wheels. This is not a necessity however. It is possible to build your home on a sturdy foundation if you don't plan on taking your tiny home to the highway.

If you'd like to one day travel with your tiny home in tow, you'll be required to understand the similar requirements to driving with a trailer. The United States, there are certain standards that must be observed for the purpose of being able to place the house in the road. For instance, the distance between the trailer and the vehicle must be no more than 60 feet and the trailer must not be more than 45 feet long. The exact measurements could differ across other parts of the world.

There is also the need to find out on the requirements for driver's licenses for driving with a trailer. In most cases it is required to have a professional driver's license is required before you can drive an automobile with a trailer tow.

Builders and contractors

Are you planning to construct the home yourself or do you require assistance to construct it? Many small home owners have built their homes, however you don't have to build it in the event that you do not wish to. If you choose to build your home yourself, ensure that you have enough time to complete the construction of your home. One last thing you'll want to do is be able to build a trailer for your backyard or foundation on a tiny lot that you purchased which you've yet to finish working on. Make sure you have the right tools and equipment to complete the DIY project for your small home.

However If you choose to employ a contractor ensure that you hire an experienced one before construction gets underway. It will also aid you with managing the project by attending a few workshops that focus on the construction of small houses.

The management of time is also crucial for this project (in any type of project in fact) since dragging out the duration of construction can lead in frustration, and eventually, a larger budget than you had hoped for.

Plumbing and electricity

Plumbing and electricity may seem quite trivial if you're aware of how a small house operates, particularly when you're looking to purchase an mobile home. If you've hired a professional to work with, plumbing and electricity will be the least of your concerns. You'll need decide on the type of electrical connection you want to use, whether traditional hookups or RV hookups solar or battery power, and water system, whether traditional plumbing well water, refillable cisterns or water hoses that connects to a conventional plumbing be, as well as where you would like the lights and plumbing fixtures located. Cooling and heating options are also part of the equation, and you'll have to think on the various options that you can make regarding this issue.

Budget

The budget, in particular it should be planned in advance. If possible, you should do it in cents, to ensure that you track the expenses you incur during the course of the undertaking. Keep in mind that the purpose of living in a small house and simplifying your life is to reduce your expenses as much possible. In contrast to conventional housing, in the smallest amount feasible, mortgages shouldn't be on your list of priorities. They will only defy the goal of living a modest life.

Chapter 13: Using Space Efficiently

Something you'll need be thinking about, especially in the event that you plan to reside in a small home, is how you can make the space the most efficient way.

Three essential items you must include inside your tiny home include an area for sleeping as well as a bath and toilet as well as the kitchen. It's a fact and you should definitely be able to have these rooms inside your tiny home regardless of the cost.

What size of room do you require for your bath and toilet? Find your body's dimensions and multiply it by three and you'll have a bathroom with all the essential features such as composting toilets (if you do not choose the flush toilet) and enough room for you to move around while you shower.

What is your kitchen like? What size of space do you really require? How many appliances do actually have and do you really require that many to be able to live comfortably. Most people find that an kitchen including a refrigerator stove, and a sink are sufficient. Making it all work without removing a significant amount of valuable real estate will be a major challenge, but it's not impossible as the owners of small homes have demonstrated over the decades.

If you prefer smaller appliances. You can have a large sink to wash your dishes as easily as you like and choose a full-sized stove or a tabletop model that is easy to put away when you are not using it. Check out the internet and local outdoor and camping store to find appliances that are compacted to fit inside the RVs and camping bags. These are the appliances that you can install at home and use comfortably without having to sacrifice space.

The last but not last thing, your bedroom. The majority of people living in tiny homes prefer to have a loft style of bedroom they can climb to at night when they're ready to go to bed. That's where the expression: "if it's not broken do not repair it" is applied. Because it appears to work for the majority of people, think about the loft-style bedroom to be your sleeping place. It may be difficult for some , but with time, once you've gotten comfortable with it the idea will get more comfortable in the end.

If there's any consolation for you that you climb from your bed should provide you a few minutes of exercise both in the morning and late at the night, leading in a greater physical fitness level at the end.

Then, decide which three spaces will be placed first, then design the rest the house in the way you think appropriate.

One method to make your small home appear bigger is to let the outside to enter. It is possible to do this by installing massive windows, which let more light into your home while doing it. It is also possible to install massive bay doors that open or slide down to open your home even more. This requires a lot of money, but the advantages that you will reap from all that free space are priceless.

A positive effect that those who live in tiny homes experience is that the longer they are in such a small space and the tighter they are conscious about their environmental footprint. The ability to be mindful and minimalistic is increased. It's impossible to have too much things in your tiny home otherwise, you'll end up with lots of clutter, and little space to move around in and, even less, live in.

Here are some additional practical ways to use space efficiently within your tiny home:

Shelves and cabinets

Installing shelves in your small home will improve the storage capacity to store your possessions. Additionally, you can install cupboards to store your possessions hidden away to keep it clutter-free.

Sliding doors

Doors that swing take up huge amount of space once they are they are opened. This could cause an intermittent blockage each time you open them. To avoid this it is possible to install sliding doors. They require less area than conventional doors and add more personality to your small home.

Furniture that can be used for multiple purposesor furniture that is concealable

Multi-functional furniture has become the norm currently for a number of tiny RV and home owners as they allow them to make the most of the space available in their homes and serve many functions for furniture items which take up lots of space even when not being used. The ability to fold them or hide the furniture in any manner can also increase the space you live in even when they're not in use , so make sure to research this.

The final decision of how to increase the area inside your small house is best determined by how creative you are. Once you've set your mind to it, you'll be able to think up a number of ideas that are great and even you can even invent methods already in place. If you've got an original idea it might be a good idea to communicate it to the other members of the tiny home community. You are sure to aid a lot of people who are scratching their heads at the moment, searching for space saving solutions.

Chapter 14: Plan For A Tiny House

1. Find a location

After deciding that a tiny house is right for you and you've completed the initial preparations, the biggest hurdle is likely be finding the right location to build your tiny home. This should be your first priority. In reality, there aren't many places in which you could put your small home legally , so you'll need to think outside the box. In order to avoid disappointment tie your place before you get overwhelmed with your home plans.

In terms of zoning there isn't a thing as an "tiny class of house". However, zoning regulations can differ greatly from one place to another location, it is highly likely that your house will not satisfy that minimum sq ft requirements for new constructions. Therefore, it is likely to fall within what is currently a gray zone. This means that even if you own your property, it might never be permitted to reside on it in the confines of your tiny home! There are many options to deal with this.

A few people who want to cut back on their spending may opt to lease out their huge home and build a smaller home in their backyard. In this case the tiny home could be considered as an accessory dwelling unit that is attached to another construction. Another possibility is reverse the procedure. Explore leasing land from a friend or family member - or anyone else who is familiar with and accepting of the idea of tiny home living.

When faced with the problem of finding a suitable location many people decide that it's a good idea to construct their home on wheels for many reasons. First, it can allow you to avoid building codes and permits that would otherwise be refused. You'll instead have to deal with the neighborhood Department of Motor

Vehicles (or the equivalent, in the area you reside).

A small house that is with wheels is usually into the category of RV, or Motor Home category (you will be more successful with this when it's not a DIY build). If it is a mobile home it is possible to live there full time, but that's but not the complete tale.

The majority of tiny home owners don't think of living in a mobile Home or an RV Park. Outside of these locations, the mobile home is considered to be temporary housing. Even if you put it on your own property, it could be considered camping even though it is not permitted, however depending on the location, you may be able be able to.

The best advice is to be in the gray zone, and do your best to stay under the radar and feel grateful that your home has wheels. If you need the need to relocate, then you have the option.

Mobility can also offer other benefits for people who don't own their own property. You might prefer having no obligation to any specific location. Additionally, if you are able to afford buying the land, you can choose to relocate your home to the new location in order to live it, or even make it an additional structure. Many owners offer their small house another life by using it as a holiday home or a home office, guest house, or an in-law room.

2. House Plan Discussions

There are a lot of options to consider before making a decision on the design concept for your home's small size.

Cost

The cost of building a tiny home will differ based on the size, materials used and the possibility of build the house yourself or buying an already-built home. A rough estimate based on the different factors would be between $23,000 and $50,000.

Create a budget first and then consider what you are able to afford or buy within this budget. Take into consideration your financial plan the fact that it will not be possible to obtain the money to build the smallest house. It will be necessary depend on credit cards, savings or a loan backed by friends or family to help you achieve this dream.

Another thing to keep when creating your budget is that even though small homes are less expensive small appliances can be more costly. Additionally, you will not benefit from economies of size when purchasing fixturesor other construction materials.

Because of this, small homes are much more costly per square foot than the larger houses. For instance, while the house that is 1,500 square feet or more weighs around 166 dollars per square feet, while a smaller home with the same features but is just 150 square feet would end in a cost of $266 per square foot.

The figures might not be relevant for those who are building their own house however, you will not be able to avoid buying small appliances. It is also important to take into consideration the expense in time and the tools you'll need, and possibly the cost renting a separate property that you can build your home. If the site you are considering isn't connected to an electrical source Don't forget to consider the expense of the purchase of a generator.

Make sure to include the price of a trailer into your budget. Based on whether you choose standard or custom, they are priced from $3,000-$7,000. The one thing that all seem to agree on is that this isn't an opportunity to save money. Along with being transportable, your trailer can be your tiny home's base.

Size

When you've created an budget, start by drawing an approximate floor plan based on the way you live. it will provide you with an idea of the size you'll need and influence your design plans.

Determine what you really want and design using this as a minimum Be aware that you've made the decision to design your home to be smaller. Tiny homes usually are between 100-500 square feet. What size would you prefer for your home?

You need to have a safe dry, warm and dry place to reside in, but you should consider how you reside and how you adapt to this. What type of seating will you require as well as where you will consume your meals, and how will you cook your meals? What are the essential appliances you cannot use? Do you work from home?

The majority of people don't bother with dishwashers in favour of extra storage space, but do you have the option of hanging your clothes outside and not need drying clothes? Consider writing down the things you do every day and write about how you conduct yourself throughout the day. Write this down.

Examine how you live your life. The best way to do this is to go through your entire week of living with a sense of mindfulness by observing your habits and habits related to trash, laundry recycling, cooking as well as food prep. Determine what you'll need to alter in your original "idea of an action plan" and consider the things you might need to change in your daily routine to achieve it (e.g. no more big gatherings or a designated workspace). Prioritizing is essential should you have to cut someplace due to costs or space constraints you'll be able to determine which cuts to make first.

If you've got a rough concept of the size of the home you'd like to buy, you'll need to decide on certain essential components that it will comprise.

Power

Decide whether to go with either way is a choice you'll have to make and must be based on the kind of appliances you require. If you intend to install an oven, fridge or water heater you'll definitely require 220. Alternately, you can utilize propane appliances and use 110 for lights and plugs.

Toilets

There is the option of using a septic system that includes regular flush toilets , or you can make use of low flush toilets for RV. There are other options to consider:

High-tech toilets that compost

Toilets that are low-tech for composting (for example, ones that utilize sawdust)

Incinerating toilets

Heating and Cooling

It is possible to heat your tiny home using propane or space heaters. The most exciting options are radiant heating flooring or a tiny wood-burning stove. You can set up an insignificant AC unit inside a small home, however those who are eco-conscious could want to think about well situated windows to catch the breeze, and then supplement them with fans that can be moved around the space.

With these ideas in your head, you are able to start putting your plans in the real world and start planning your small home.

Chapter 15: What to Maximize the Value Of A Small Living Space Small House Plans

There are numerous ways to design small-sized houses to maximize the space that is available. These techniques are crucial in communities with limited space. A lot of architects who design strategies for smaller homes are aware of the methods of business that make spaces appear larger. However, the homeowner should also be informed about the various methods and various options to design the interior to ensure the most out of the small home plans.

One of the most common features of small home plans is the attempt to design the space to appear bigger than the specific dimensions of the space. One of the most effective square footage that developers consider for square footage for small homes strategies is to construct tall ceilings, which makes an impression of greater space regardless of how.

There are many design sources that a homeowner can utilize to highlight this aspect. The owner could create an horizontal line through the room and paint the upper half with a lighter hue and the lower half the area a darker shade. This gives the impression of a more top. Homeowners can further enhance their small house plans by acquiring small pictures that could be connected in size and then positioned in a straight line in a prominent location to the wall. This brings the focus at the vertical point rather than the dimensions or dimensions and creates an impact.

Another thing that homeowners must consider when deciding on the best method to implement their small home plans is how to store furniture.

A large, overstuffed sofa can be a great thing but when it's put in a smaller space, it can become overwhelming. It is crucial to consider the possibilities, and that every inch counts. Decorating the rooms too much can help with the dimensions while the excessive decoration could highlight the tiny size of the area that homeowners need to be wary of. The best approach to design for smaller-sized house plans could be to keep the furniture and decor to a to a minimum.

The furniture must also be adjustable in the height. A huge lamppost next to the chair will make the sofa appear more manageable. Instead of a large bookcase that consumes space, owners must utilize cabinets to store their books which change in height, making space and creating the visual illusion of

In the present difficult economic times, lots of people are seeking high-performance living. One method to get there could be to design small home plans that will work. It's crucial to plan each square inch of space to ensure luxurious and powerful results when building small home plans. This approach must start with you as the homeowner.

Every person has a desire for their home and has a variety of desires. It's not easy to prove that an energy efficient home, in terms of energy usage however, it's not for every person. A benefit of smaller houses is they permit you to build with energy efficiency in an important factor. There are a variety of components that can be focused on to improve efficiency.

One location that can create huge impact are windows and openings. A smaller house plan typically has fewer windows and chances, which are often the most costly components of a house. By reducing opportunities and windows, you are capable of sticking to your the budget. Windows and doors could be where much heat (or cooling) is missing, so by lowering them you need to make use of a smaller

HVAC (heating/ventilation/AC) system, thereby saving money. In smaller homes, HVAC products may be smaller and more efficient due to the fact that they do not have the ability to cool or heat the vast house. The effectiveness could be improved at a an affordable cost because of the smaller size of the area.

One of the most important things to take into consideration is the manner in which you plan to utilize the space. Consider issues such as an media room in your exercise room or even a home workplace. You might want to think about the future growth of the family, and you will require more rooms. It is worth thinking about reselling the property. A lot of us construct the dream house we envision could be our forever home However, needs as well as family and career plans shift. Remember that many people are contemplating not less than three bedrooms or two bathrooms. This could allow you to to draw a wider range of potential buyers when you need to sell your home.

Here are some aspects to consider when creating a small home plan that you should keep in your mind:

A sketch is designed to show the outside edge (sitting space) of the countertop in the kitchen that is round. It could double as a dining table.

Pocket doors are ideal for smaller homes, particularly for use in modern contemporary homes. These space-saving possibilities does not provide an individual look but a actuality. The home is preserved because of the absence of an "move" area to put doors is a nightmare. Pocket doors cost nothing for the creator to put in but in a small home, they can alter lives.

3. When properly put in place. It is essential to limit them to no more than what is feasible, as activities can be large and can be a major eater of space and can

be uncomfortable, but allow for a saferesidence and size measurements to move furniture. Spiral stairs take little space, but they can be dangerous and difficult to operate. The storage area under traditional stairs can be extremely significant.

4. Raise your ceiling height. This is a cost-effective way to make your website appear bigger than they actually are. The average ceiling height of 8 feet. However, you've got a substantial amount of overall and space look at a very low cost, in the event that it increases to 9 or even 12 feet. Include floor-to-floor fans to circulate air, and ceiling units to store items.

5. If you are looking for a small two-story house designs, you could consider an gambrel roof. These are the best styles you see on older barns. They provide a large roof space and more ground space than the typical roof.

There's usually a wide array of modern house-keeping tools and techniques that homeowners can avail. When you are thinking ahead and conducting the necessary research, you are capable of expanding your house to meet your needs.

Chapter 16: Designing A Tiny House

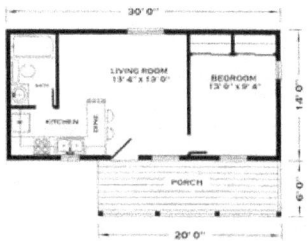

Design is the very first step in building your very own home. It is important to understand that designing a tiny house is very different from creating the typical size home, even though certain procedures are similar. To design your home for small spaces efficiently, follow these easy steps:

Find out the exact type of tiny house you'd like to live in.

You can begin the process of building a home without knowing the exact specifications you'd like. For instance, some prefer a small home that is mobile, while others would prefer a smaller home on their own property with a solid base. In the same way someone else might want the privacy of a small area to use for personal purposes, and another person might require a smaller home where they can host a meal with a handful of acquaintances. All of these choices will help determine the design of your house. Before you begin designing your home , take note of your needs and then decide what you require for your house.

The answers to the question "what do I require in an apartment that is small?" can assist you in designing the house that you've always dreamed of but only if those answers are truthful. Be truthful in every response you provide and look to see what you feel like when you think about living in the space you're considering. In the beginning of designing, is the best time to determine the space you will need for in terms of floor space as well as that for your bedroom. The process of determining what you actually need could be a lengthy process that can take months, weeks, perhaps even years. It is possible to test various things when living in a smaller area before you're certain about what you want and require.

Make a list of everything you'll be bringing into your new home.

It includes things like pets and family members. in addition, you must include physical items such as kitchen appliances furniture, bathroom essentials, furniture clothes and so on. In a small home they will require storage space. The presence of a large amount of clutter makes the house appear cramped. So, you should take your home goods down to the extent you can. Then, design your space to fit the items you decide to put in. The design you create of the way you'll keep items is essential for the overall layout of your home.

Start where you want to in your design process:

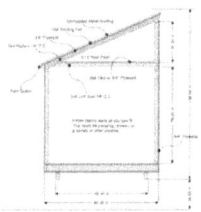

Nowadays with lots of small home designs for free available online, you can modify an existing design online , or start from the blank start. Making use of an existing design can greatly reduce the amount of work you have to do and enable you to design the best home design within the shortest amount of time. If you're looking to build around the design of someone else, make sure you browse the internet to find something that truly resonates with you. By using a style that you like, you'll be better positioned to create the perfect tiny house style that meets your requirements.

There are a lot of tiny home plans there. If you don't find one that is able to meet the needs of your family I would suggest you begin with a blank start. It can be difficult to make adjustments to an existing house style. This is because the parts of a tiny house are typically particular to the people who created the house. Modifying or moving one component could affect many others and, in some cases create a situation that makes the rest in the form less ideal.

Start with a clean start will allow you the ability to create your own ideas and create your home to satisfy your requirements. This eliminates the hassle of trying to figure out ways to place items in areas that weren't designed to accommodate such things. Making decisions from a blank slate will also mean that you're not in the direction of others. It is all too easy for our minds get influenced by thoughts of others. If you're looking to design a small house that represents your personality, and who you are, then you shouldn't examine the designs of others. This will allow you to create a tiny home design that truly yours.

You may want to consider the use of design software to make your work simpler:

There are many design tools that will aid you in a simple and quick way to make your home small. For instance, you could utilize Google Sketch Up to design your tiny home using three dimensions. It is a great tool for creating floor plans, when you are designing your walls , and for creating the head room or other specific structures. There are many other programs available on the web that you can utilize to help you work. Choose a design program that you can easily comprehend and use it to design the perfect home style for your tiny house.

Sketching your Tiny House Floor Plan

Floor plans are an essential element of a tiny home design. Learning how to sketch the floorplan is essential because it can help to communicate your ideas in crystal precise terms for the construction of your home in a small space. To create a great floor plan, follow these easy steps:

Begin by addressing the obvious

The best place to begin is drawing the floor's outer shape. It is essential to understand the total needs of your floor and the shape, and then work on it. Drawing a floor's outline will allow you to understand how to organize the floor area so you can use the space more efficiently. Then, you can increase the floor space by adding essential elements of your home like the kitchen as well as the dining space. This allows you to build on additional crucial areas to become covered in the floor. To aid you with this there are many tools for designing architectural structures like AutoCAD or Sketch Up which can in drawing the layout much more easily.

Many small home architects have found the Sketch Up very useful. It is a sketch Up is a no-cost 3D design software that is easy to master. With this program, you can sketch out the floor plan, as well as the complete three-dimensional plan as well as crucial elements of your tiny home. Instructional guides can be found via the internet as well as Michael Janzen from Tiny House Design has created an extremely helpful video-based instructional program to guide you designing your home.

Understanding the dimensions of the various objects

To create a clear layout of your floor space you must determine the dimensions of the houses you'll have to accommodate in your tiny home. For instance, in the kitchen area, you have to determine the dimensions of the kitchen appliances so that you can divide the floor space of your kitchen with appliances in your mind. In addition, the kitchen is likely to have cabinets and a work desk you need to consider. It is also important to determine the dimensions that your table as well as bed in order to determine how you can allocate the floor space. Furniture is a big part of the space, so you must know what furniture you'll need for your tiny home so that you have adequate space. Bathrooms are also a crucial element of any home. When you design your small home, be aware of the building code requirements for toilets and bathrooms. It is crucial to make sure your home that is built to meet the requirements.

Create for the walls, windows and doors

The thickness of windows and doors affects the floor plan and how you organize your possessions within your tiny home. Wall thickness can take up spaces in your tiny house and it is crucial to think about it when drawing floor plans. The size of the door and its location significantly affect the way you utilize the floor space in your tiny house. The typical size of doors

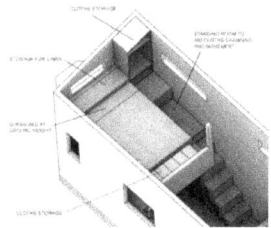

for residential properties is 3-4" that you must include in your floor layout. This will help you maximize the use of your floor space.

Designs for Specific Features

There are many additional special features that could impact your floor's layout. Design for plumbing walls or solar design, and also shear walls. When planning your interior, you must consider crucial factors like the location of your plumbing pipes as well as water requirements.

Create the Elevation

When you're done with the floor, the next step is to draw the elevation of your tiny home. The elevation is the front look of your tiny home. It is important to consider both the elevations of the interior and exterior of your home. This is crucial in helping to determine the height and the way your tiny home will look. Include both the front elevation as well as the side elevation of your home.

In order to draw your elevation, you must consider the most important elevations of your home including the ground level elevation, the floor's finished elevation, second-floor elevation, the top wall plate, the top floor elevation, the counter in your kitchen and roof's top elevation. This is crucial to ensure that you draw a more accurate elevation sketch of your tiny home.

In the course of designing your elevation it is your responsibility to play around to the design of your home , both outdoors and inside to create the perfect style of your house.

Create the Cross-section

The cross-section of your tiny house is another crucial design element that you need to focus on. The cross section is your vertical plane of your house cut in such a way that you can view it as it looks from above. This image will provide an idea of how your home will appear. Be sure to take note of every important element of your house when making the cross-sectional view since this will let you understand how the various elements like your bed, as well as the kitchen cupboard will be placed within your home.

Design the 3D Model

If you already have a kitchen design as well as a cross-section and the elevations of your house you must be able to create 3D models to aid you in building your home. There are numerous computer programs that will help you to create a 3D representation of your home's tiny dimensions. For instance Sketch Up that is a no-cost design software can assist you in creating a precise 3D model of your home.

It is also possible to build an actual model of your dream home. This could be a bit time-consuming, but it will help you comprehend the issues you'll face when you build your tiny house. It is easy to build a model of your home using cardboard. It is essential to be aware of the tiny details to are aware of how the various components of your home can be put together.

Tiny Kitchen Design

In a world where tiny homes shrink in size, finding enough space for efficient kitchens becomes even more difficult. If you have a good design, however it's possible to design your kitchen to meet the needs of your daily diet. The installation of a gas stove with two burners along with a large refrigerator and countertop space counters to store your food and even a small work area connects to the counter in your kitchen requires an appropriate design. The trick to making smaller kitchens for houses is to layout them so that they can be used for the kitchen, as well as to have a bathroom in the same area of the home.

The best way to save money and space in a small kitchen is to use non-standard cabinets and counters. Standard cabinets will consume a lot of space, which isn't needed. The majority of lower cabinets are a bit deep enough that they occupy a significant amount of space at the back isn't usable. If you don't have to store lots of things, you'll be fine with cabinets that are small. A kitchen that is functional is a perfect choice for couples who enjoy dining out several times per week. They can also cook your own meals up to 3-4 times per week. It is essential to include two burners, for instance, which is essential to supply vital nutrition to the residents of the tiny house.

In combining a kitchen and lavatory into one "wing" in a tiny house, it can save plenty of space. In particular, the extra space can be used to store many other things.

Chapter 17: Strategies and Strategies For Living In A Small House

If you now have a plan of the best way to proceed with this, you should start to "try" the way tiny homes operate, just to gain a sense of what they do and see how you and your family could adapt to the idea. To do this, you need be aware of the following aspects:

Take a look at your life style as well as your family's size. Do you have children who have to attend school? Do you regularly invite guests over or host extravagant events? Do you think that you'll be capable of making the change without having an issue?

Take a look at some excursion lodges. You should lease at least one of them. They'll provide you with a sense of what a tiny home is. Once you're in you'll be able to evaluate the advantages and disadvantages of living in a tiny house. You'll begin to realize the challenges of moving in a small space and then determine if really like it or if it's not the right choice for you. In this way, you will not spend time moving if you aren't sure it would be a good fit for you, and also make you feel comfortable regardless of the reason.

You should ensure that there is lots of open air and space. If you choose to reside in a tiny home, you'll have ensure that plenty of air will be available and not be restricted or confined in any manner. It is possible to search for homes that are situated in the entryway, or that have large areas of land and decks that wrap around.

Allow utilities to flow. The issue with tiny homes is that they need simple ways to connect to services like running water or power, as well as sewerage. It is essential to be able to integrate these services into your home. Consider whether you'll have internet connectivity, and if you are able to use the water systems of oriental origin. It is essential to know how to evaluate your surroundings and determine what you could do with it, and what will help you.

You must ensure that you comply with the zoning/construction regulations. It's an injustice to build an apartment and be forced to tear it down due to the fact that you haven't examined the Zoning or construction laws. Whatever the size of your home may be there are laws that must be adhered to. Ensure that you're aware of them.

Have less. Clear the clutter from your home and determine which items you need to throw out. If you think you have items that others could benefit from, you can give them away or donate them. Get rid of things you haven't used for a while, you can always manage with just one or two clothes. Do not let the idea of being too "sentimental" make you the kind of person who is a hoarder. A tiny home will definitely seem spacious without the extra clutter within your home.

Do Less. The issue is not being lazy or even being an irritable. Most of the time, it has to do with the ability to complete a lot of work in a short amount of time. Quality is more important than quantity, as they claim. Cut down on your to-do list as well as your work load and your responsibilities. Reduce the number of activities on your calendar. Do you really need to attend the family reunion every week? Do you have to go to the same party every Friday evening? It's about understanding what your priorities are and then deciding to put your focus on them, and not on the things that aren't important in your life. Take it slowly and you'll notice the positive results on you.

Create Less. Enhance the quality of your life and the things you already are, instead of making things you've no idea how to be useful. Be aware of the things is already in your life, value themand make the most of their value. Be careful not to create excessive noise and tension in your life. You'll only get stressed out this way. Concentrate on what you do and do your best at what you must accomplish. The rest will follow soon.

Avoid spending your time online. If your job isn't online, keep in mind that you are entitled to choose to avoid the social media platform too often. Sometimes, what you read online can affect your mood, or affect the way you feel. And if you're stressed out this can be detrimental to your health. Make time for other activities such as writing, rather than blogging, go out, go to the movies and movies, take a break from reading books, and give yourself time to experience the real world, not in being in the virtual world every day.

Consume less! Do not feel that you have to have everything to be happy in this world. If you already have the things you require and want, you will feel more content when you begin to appreciate them instead of dwelling on what you feel you don't have. Don't focus on the things you do not have, and you'll feel much more satisfied.

Do not forget to consider the place you are staying in.

The position of your home's tiny footprint must also be among your primary concerns. Zoning restrictions must be taken into consideration however, aside from that, you should be aware of the following aspects:

Fabricated Homes

If you've built a home, or one that is located in one place then you can look at these locations:

Wee Casa--Colorado. There are currently 10 lots in this area that are available for rent, however only for short-term for living reasons. That means that you will need to relocate in three to six months.

Portland Garden Cottages - Oregon. It is possible to rent lots here for as little as a month. But you need to call as soon as you can because there are only a limited lots available. And they are intended for smaller tiny houses , which have a maximum of the size of 364 sq ft.

Getaway House in New Hampshire. In addition to lot rentals You can also take advantage of amenities for community getaways (i.e. food, snacks, activities) and showers and toilets that compost. So you don't have to install them inside your home.

Dignity Village--Oregon. If you are a poor person then you should look for parking within Dignity Village in Oregon as rents are affordable throughout the year. They currently have approximately 60 residents.

Blue Moon Rising in Maryland. This eco-friendly resort has land available for rental of 275-400 square feet. They also have tiny homes which can house up to four people.

RV Parks

Naturally, you could also consider RV Parks, or places you could place your RV tiny house. It could be any of the below:

Pine Acres Campground - South Carolina. The campground can be found at the address the address 205 Duke Drive, Aiken, South Carolina. It is essential to ensure that your tiny home has only 30/50 amps of power to be able to lease the land.

Oceanside Beachfront RV Resort - Oregon. It is a peaceful environment for tiny home owners across the globe. To reserve rentals and reservations go to the park's address: 90281 Cape Arago Highway, Coos Bay, Oregon.

Hidden Acres Family Campground--Virginia. Another place you can stay! It is located in 17391 Richard Turnpike, Milford, Bowling Green, Virginia.

Evergreen RV Park--California. It Park is found at 2135 Oxnard Boulevard located in Oxnard, California. The park will accept small homes which are RVIA certified or have accreditation through the Recreation Vehicle Industry Association.

Creekside RV Park and Cain Plantation, Georgia. This is possibly one of the easiest parks to park at as it doesn't require any announcements nor RVIA certifications. The park can be found at the 6143 U.S. Highway 41 North, Hahira, Georgia.

Campground Creek N Wood in New York. It's another location to stay at with no certification or notices are required! The location is in 2528 Wheeler Station Road, East Bloomfield, New York.

Cloudbase RV Park--Tennessee. It is among the most well-known RV parks across the United States. The only issue is that it's nearly always full, so be sure to go there and reserve a spot prior to your visit. It's located in the southern end of Chattanooga close to Wildwood, Georgia.

Christmas RV Park in Florida. It's not just accessible during the Christmas season; it is open throughout the year. All you have to do is make sure your home can be RVIA certified. You can find this RV Park located at the address 25525 E. Colonial Drive, Christmas, Florida.

All Seasons RV Park in California. The park is located near Interstate 15 Exit 41, they also allow tiny homes which have been approved from the RVIA. It is also recommended to provide them with one month's notice prior to placing your tiny home there.

If you're the type of person who is minimalist, or you are aware that you'll be moving around often, it could be best to rent the space you need for your tiny home. Start by looking at the examples above, or search for one close to your house.

Chapter 18: What's the reason for a Tiny House? Pros And Cons.

As I've already said it is not for everyone to appreciate and feel comfortable with the concept being in the midst of a small home. In a country where the average home is two hundred square feet living with a footprint of 160 square feet could be a snide idea to some.

All it boils down to the most basic requirements of every human being: food, water and shelter. In the language of our modern times, that is four walls and roof, a space to sleep, a space in which you can wash yourself and cook your meals, the provision of running water that is clean, and a means by where people can dispose of the waste. The rest of what we are surrounded by is considered a luxury, not essential.

The appeal to living in such a smaller home is that it can provide all these amenities and amenities, but still enjoys some of the amenities you normally find in a big home. In addition it makes sure that owners aren't slapped with the same cost or environmental impact. If you don't have to worry about, you have more time to enjoy the things you like to do!

In French the word "mortgage" literally refers to "death agreement." A majority of homeowners end up spending 30 years paying for their homes, the ultimate cost being two times than the initial cost due to interest. The housing market is always the most expensive expense, however it's not always the case to be this the way.

The time and money that is spent making payments on a mortgage could be better spent in different directions. You can create exciting new memories together with loved ones than confined in an office - after all, you only live once!

One of the primary reasons you should consider with a small dwelling is that it sets you apart from the race. Your footprint on the environment is drastically reduced as you reside in a small home. The reality is beginning to become apparent to those who live there that there is a lot of damage that has been done to the planet and a change is required.

Downsizing is a way towards the right direction. Recycled and reclaimed materials are being increasingly utilized to build tiny houses. Smaller sizes mean an energy consumption that is lower that can be managed by some solar panels. Being eco-friendly citizens is another reason we must adjust to living in tiny.

A tiny home has its fair number of drawbacks. There is no debate regarding this. The lack of space is one of the main issues but it could be seen as a blessing as it will limit you to the items you own, and there will be no room to spend money on unnecessary things.

In the age of space-saving chores like cleaning your home can get quicker. Instead of letting your possessions take over your life it is now your turn to exert control over your possessions. You'll be required to think about what you could bring home with an item that is merely packaging or a fast food container that could cause a rapid mess.

The residents of tiny homes have to be accountable and recycle whatever they can. For those who are hoarders living in a tiny house is almost impossible! For a person who is just one could find a tiny home as a great option, even though families may face challenges. This type of house is not ideal for couples due its lack of privacy, but when they have a better understanding of each other, things could work just perfectly.

Why should we say "YES" for a small home?

Lower Interest Costs to Pay

If you purchase a brand new home, you typically will end up paying more in interest than is the actual amount. It's no secret that in the course of a 30-year loan, the interest payable is greater than the cost of the property the property. For the majority of homeowners with tiny homes opt to pay cash or to pay off the loan amount as swiftly as they can. At the end of the day, the amount that is saved by the concept of interest is an enormous amount. It is enough to purchase an additional tiny home for your in-laws , and to have it placed at the back very back of your property!

Additional Disposable Income

Although all the reasons mentioned so far were focused upon the "less" aspect but they all are all a way of increasing the amount of money in your pockets. If you take an annual list of your expenses you'll discover that the bulk of your expenses are incurred by your house, and that they account for the largest portion of your expenses every day. Living in a small house can cut down on your costs of living at nearly every degree.

Less Food

A small pantry means that it is easier to store food in a smaller amount. that can be kept in the home decreases. If you have fresh veggies growing in your garden and you are able to spend less on purchasing produce at the market. In a smaller amount of food consumed within your home's small space, you will be able to keep your weight and your food expenses at a minimum.

Taxes to pay less

Because the small home and the land it sits on aren't as significant, the tax burden will be lower as well. It is possible to put your savings for investment, donations, vacations or education for your kids or for planning your retirement.

Less Repair Costs

The cost of repair for small homes is more than simple math. The expense of replacing the roof on a home of 2000 square feet will be significantly higher than 300 square feet of home because of the lower the cost of labor and materials.

The less land required for purchase and upkeep

A small home will require considerably less land to build on. Since many cities have limitations regarding the size of homes and the size of a home, it is possible to buy land outside of the city limits, where there aren't any restrictions. In this case, not only is the land less expensive, but you have to pay less tax. With a small piece of land available for your house it is possible to reduce the time spent cutting the grass, but have enough space to build an outdoor garden.

Less Initial Cost

It is a given that a tiny home is less than a conventional home. It requires lesser materials and labor due to its dimensions. A majority of the elements of traditional homes are found in tiny houses including flooring, roofing plumbing, kitchen and many more. Therefore, the price per square foot is likely to be quite expensive. But, as the total size is extremely small, it is only one-third of the cost of buying a conventional home.

A slender amount of insurance to invest in

Insurance for your home could be quite costly particularly when you're making use of it. Insurance for tiny homes is considerably less due to the lesser value that comes with it. Many insurance companies also classify tiny homes on wheels to be RV. Since insurance companies are non-profit organisations that are in business of making money, separating your debts from them could be an extremely difficult job. The tiny size of your house can decrease the amount you're legally required to pay in the beginning.

Reduced Energy Consumption

A small home will require less energy to heat and cooling due to the fact that the inside air space is so tiny. Since a large portion of these houses being on wheels, it's possible for the homeowner to move the house beneath an immense tree in summer and to the sun in winter.

Refrigerators and hot water heaters are the two biggest energy users in any home. In tiny homes, they're smaller and use less energy. Also, you will make use of less of your own energy as the area to be maintained and cleaned is tiny.

Reduced water consumption and less trash

With a tiny shower and a tiny water heater installed it is possible to assume that showers will last significantly smaller than. In addition, with a tiny trash can , the amount of produced waste is less. Utilizing less water and producing less trash is great for the environment but also good for your pocket.

Decluttering

An untidy home can bring more problems than you could ever imagine! Are you interested in taking an examination of some problems you're likely to be dealing with because of your messed up and unorganized home? Check it out!

Clutter refers to a lot of unneeded or old things that may not be even in your awareness are located in your home. This takes up a lot space that you could make use of to store the useful things that end up scattered throughout the home.

As more mess notice and feel around, the more anxiety you feel. Every day you are thinking about how to clean up your environment and so you lose the opportunity to take a break!

The energy and time you use up trying to tidy your messy surroundings could be better utilized for a different exercise.

After you've cleared out certain things, you can begin looking at the different rooms of your home and figure out how you can make your space better than ever. There are certainly some fantastic techniques and tricks you wouldn't have thought of (but they do turn out well).

If you're spending the majority of your time trying searching for items you lost in your home, like keys, bank cards , or your phone and more, it's time to clean your home! If you're overwhelmed by stacks of papers and books as well as piles of items which you don't know what to do with and then it becomes difficult to decide where to begin the clean-up.

So , get ready to take off the clutter in your home and stop it from coming back by using these easy-to-follow tips and tricks that will motivate you to get started now!

Start small! A home that's encased in the mess can be difficult to tidy up. It's important to be prepared for a long period of effort and begin by working on a smaller scale!

Clean out your drawers, give away the items you don't need and, If you'd like, organize an event to get rid of all the rubbish. Use small containers inside your drawers to organize small things such as hairpinsand paperclips etc.

The desks are often the most messy area in the room. Small pieces of paper, old receipts , coins, bills and other things cover every inch of your desk. Begin by creating stacks of the floor with similar things. For example, a stack of money you may be able to find in the kitchen, in trash important notes, etc. Recycling all paper that is not needed and dispose of the trash.

• Walk through the house with the laundry basket and take all the dirty clothes scattered around! Sort the darks from the brights and put them in the washing machine! When you're not able to find the space for a dryer make a clothesline in your backyard. It'll be helpful.

Eco-friendly and safety

The fundamental definition of a tiny house is that it is constructed from materials that aren't just considered to be renewable butalso are eco-friendly also. In this regard, tiny houses are an ideal choice for towns and cities who are seeking to build houses that offer eco-friendly options in the housing sector.

Based on a survey carried out by TinyHouseBuild.com the website dedicated to providing information on the construction of tiny homes The construction of a conventional house requires three-quarters of an acre of wood, which equals seven full logging trucks which provide materials. However the construction materials used in tiny homes are equivalent to half a the size of a logging truck.

Another advantage of tiny homes is that they can reduce energy usage too. An average house within the United States requires 12,733 kilowatts of power every year and releases approximately 1,144 tons of carbon dioxide on a per-year basis.

Many tiny houses get its utilities, sewerage, and water supply that traditional homes do that is by connecting to electric grids as well as other utilities that are public. But, this is carried out only in the event that the municipality or community in question allows the use of this method. If not, the tiny home can use solar panels or standard generators, or a combination of both to provide sources of energy. Water sources could include rainwater treatment or well which can also include the function of filtering the water , and heating it with the propane heating system for water.

In terms of the sewage system There are a variety of choices available. Many small-scale homeowners opt for composting toilets that utilize the natural process of decomposition, as well as the process of evaporation to remove garbage. Another option is to use incinerator toilets, which use the capability of burning waste instead of flushing them away. Additionally, some individuals may opt for septic systems, or use an elimination system for tanks that are very similar to the one the portable toilets that are being utilized.

Conclusion

Living small requires changes to your self. If there's one guiding principle you learn from this book, it is that you should get to understand yourself better.

When you're unable to sit front of someone else and tell them about who you are, the strengths and flaws you may have and also be honest about your character, free of criticism, being small is not easy.

It's about being transparent with yourself about what you are able and can't stand. If you aren't aware of your strengths or don't appreciate criticism, then if you share your tiny home with a stranger isn't going to be able to communicate in the way you require to succeed.

All the rules on how to reduce your size using the correct construction materials, and go off grid, and park your tiny home,